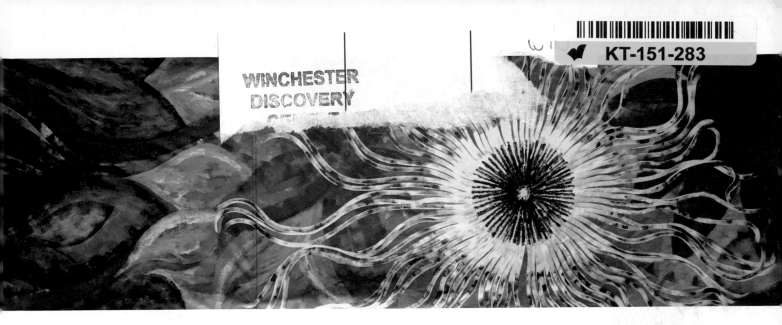

A Passion for Winchester

edited by G. Howard Mellor

Special thanks to all the lecturers from the 'Presenting the Passion' symposium at the University of Winchester for allowing us to print transcripts of their talks. We are particularly grateful to Kevin Crossley-Holland for giving us permission to reprint not only the text of his lecture on 'The Cross Crucified', but also his translation of 'The Dream of The Rood' in full, in addition to selections from several of his other published works.

Photographs throughout the book are reproduced by kind permission of Roger Brooks, Joe Low, the BBC, the Hampshire Chronicle, Ewen Huffman, Julia Hedgecoe, William Dorling, Katie Williams and a number of other photographers.

The illustration from The Winchester Troper on page 23 was provided by Dr C. de Hamel, Librarian of the Parker Library, and is reproduced by kind permission of the Master and Fellows of Corpus Christi College, Cambridge.

The photograph of the Ruthwell Cross on page 70 is copyright Doug Houghton, www.doughoughton.com.

The lyrics to 'Keep You In Peace' are © Sarah Morgan 1992.

The lyrics to 'When You're Far From Home' by June Boyce-Tillman are reprinted from 'A Rainbow To Heaven' by permission of Stainer & Bell.

The banners which have been reproduced as chapter headings were designed and made for the Winchester Passion by Helene Bevan.

Inside front cover: photograph by Alex Fyfe.
Inside back cover: painting by Derek Butler.

Many thanks to Judith Blake for the creative design and careful typesetting of this book for Sarsen Press, Winchester; to Philip Glassborow for endless ideas and Sophie Armstrong for reading the text, they saved me from countless errors and omissions, though I must be held responsible for any blemishes which remain. *HM*

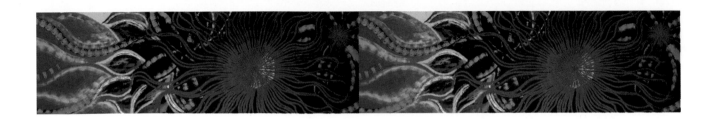

Contents

Rehearsals took place in a number of different locations around the town, including houses, halls and churches. But the only space big enough to accommodate some of the staging was an open barn in Crab Wood, kindly loaned to us by the farmer. This picture shows Geoffrey Burnaby, director of the second act scenes (top left) with his valiant cast dressed as warmly as possible against the Winchester winds.

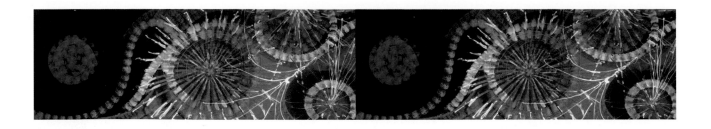

Foreword

The Bishop of Winchester
Michael Scott-Joynt

Many of us who were privileged to experience the Winchester Passion in the cold and damp of the early evening of Good Friday 2008 will find that this finely produced book stimulates our memories of a most striking event and a remarkable achievement, and lets us see something of all that lay before and behind those four hours.

I hope that many others, who perhaps live many miles from Winchester, will value the book not only for its picture of an evening that when they finish the book they may be sorry to have missed, but for what it tells of a bold initiative by a small group of the leaders of the churches of Winchester and of the marvellous response they received from church members and from so many others.

Above all, I hope that all who read it will be brought freshly face to face, as were many of the thousands of us on the streets of Winchester that night, with Jesus of Nazareth in the events of the last evening and day of his earthly life.

As a Christian, and as Bishop of Winchester, I had naturally spent Good Friday in churches, commemorating with fellow-Christians the Passion, the suffering and death, of Jesus, and seeking with words to enable us to find the figure at the heart of the stories present among us to call, challenge and empower us today.

But then in the evening the suffering and death of Jesus, and much of what led up to it, was acted out, not in churches but on the streets of Winchester; not shut up in the Bible, or available only to those who go to Church, but in the places where we live our daily lives.

There was Jesus, and the terrorist Barabbas too, in Oram's Arbour just above the railway-station, our gateway to London and to the rest of the country – and to so many people's everyday working lives.

There was the 'turning' of Judas Iscariot, Jesus' Last Supper with his friends, and Judas betraying him, outside the Great Hall which speaks of 800 years of the political history of England not just of Winchester, and close to the County Council buildings that are critical to almost every aspect of life in Hampshire.

Jesus was tried before Herod and Pilate outside the Law Courts, a powerful reminder of the violence and crime, the prisons and the asylum hostels and the penal policy, that today sum up both our characteristic human sinfulness and our equally human struggle to reflect God's justice. And all of it in expressively contemporary dress . . .

And then, after Jesus had carried his cross down the High Street and into the Cathedral Close where on a summer's day hundreds of mostly quite young people sit or lie in the sun and eat their sandwiches, the crucifixion of Jesus and of the two thieves took place on the Cathedral's West Front, and there Mary Magdalene met him after his Resurrection – with thousands of us filling that open space around the War Memorials.

I remembered that the last time I was part of such a big crowd that had walked there through the city (though the crowd on Good Friday was much bigger) was in February 2003, when people of many faiths and none gathered to say that the then-imminent War in Iraq would be 'wrong, profoundly unwise and widely damaging'. No wonder that on this Good Friday, for me, Jesus' **'Father, forgive them . . .'** was among the most convicting moments of the evening.

It was all a remarkable achievement; and I am very grateful that I could be there among the crowd . . .

+Michael Winton:

Introduction

G. Howard Mellor

Letting the story of Jesus loose on the streets of the city

The Winchester Passion was performed in the streets of Winchester on Good Friday, 21 March 2008. It was the fruit of a hitherto-unprecedented collaboration between the churches of the city, including Winchester Cathedral, and an extraordinary number of other participants. These ranged from organizations – such as the University of Winchester, BBC Radio Solent and BBC South Today, Hampshire County Council and Winchester City Council, Winchester Community Choir, Southern Voices and Waynflete Singers, and the British Army and Navy – to a great number of dedicated individuals.

To enable such an event to take place inevitably requires a vast array of technicians, costume designers and makers, stewards, lighting and sound experts, actors, singers and choirs, dancers, artists, designers for the publicity, camera crews and many more. Eight people, the 'Producers', met every week for eighteen months to guide the policy and process. Forty 'Directors', each looking after a slice of the preparation, met monthly, and altogether some 800 people delivered the most ambitious free theatrical event ever to hit the city.

We estimate the number at 800 because they are the ones we actually know about by name, but, for instance, in distributing invitation leaflets door-to-door, some parish churches only gave us one name and offered their team of visitors to ensure that every household in the city and surrounding area received an invitation through their door.

In all, some six hundred people actually took part in the presentation that evening, and the audience attendance was estimated by the police at 12,000. The entire three-hour event was broadcast live on BBC Radio Solent and was also available via the BBC's website.

In the run-up to the performance, a symposium and study day was held on 23 February 2008 at the University of Winchester entitled 'Presenting The Passion'. Jointly sponsored by Space In the City, the University and the Winchester Passion team, and with invaluable support from The Coggan Fund, it featured several practitioners and experts in different aspects of communicating the passion narrative. The intention was to offer an historical perspective to dramatizations of the story, and also to reflect on ways the challenge had been taken up in more recent times through the media of television and film.

The morning session was entitled 'From a Dream to the Street: The Passion in the Saxon and Medieval periods' and included Kevin Crossley-Holland's talk on 'The Dream of the Rood'; Canon David Scott's lecture on the earliest-known 'passion play' within church liturgy; and Martial Rose's illustrated talk on the Medieval Mysteries in performance, iconography and art.

Space in the City and The Winchester Passion warmly invite you to a one-day symposium including lectures, performance and film:

Presenting the Passion

Adam Kemp
BBC Commissioning Editor, Arts, Performance & Religion
Televising the Manchester Passion and Easter 2008

Kevin Crossley-Holland
Whitbread Award-winning author of the Arthur trilogy
The Dream of the Rood: A Passion Poem

Dr Cecily O'Neill
Author of Process Drama, Arts and Education Consultant
Staging the Winchester Passion, 2008

Norman Stone
Emmy Award-winning director of BBCtv's Shadowlands
Man Dancin'– A Contemporary Passion Movie

Martial Rose
Former Principal of King Alfred's College, Winchester
Medieval Mysteries: Iconography and Art

David Scott
Priest of St Lawrence's Church, poet and playwright
The Anglo-Saxon Passion of Winchester

The Stripe Theatre, University of Winchester
10am to 5pm,
Saturday 23 February 2008

Tickets £8.00 including lunch
from Wells Bookshops or
Winchester Cathedral Box Office 01962 857275
www.winchester-cathedral.org.uk

www.thewinchesterpassion.org.uk

Lorna Browne (centre) with some of her staging team at the Great Hall

Ken Liddell (Technology Director) and Vince Smith testing microwave camera transmission

The afternoon session was entitled 'The Shock of the Reel – The Passion in TV and film, stage and street in the 20th and 21st centuries'. This included a presentation by Adam Kemp (BBC Television's Commissioning Editor for Arts, Music, Performance and Religion) on televising the Manchester Passion and other religious programming; a seminar on 'Staging the Winchester Passion' from Dr Cecily O'Neill and Philip Glassborow; and a talk by award-winning filmmaker Norman Stone on the themes of the passion in his film and television productions. This book includes some of the lectures and talks given at the symposium, as well as additional articles on aspects of the Passion.

Our Passion became an idea as a result of watching the Manchester Passion on BBC3 on Good Friday evening 2006. It was the inspiration which galvanized us to consider the possibility that such an event was possible in Winchester. Not to replicate the event of Manchester, but to take the story of Jesus and play it out in the public space of this remarkable city. This would be *The Winchester Passion*, a church-inspired community event in which anyone could participate and all could attend free of charge. It became a vision which quickly caught the imagination not only of of the church leaders and members but also significant partners in the local community. One thing would remain non-negotiable; this Winchester Passion would be based on the gospel narrative. Of course someone needed to lift the story off the page and make it live, and we were very fortunate to discover Philip Glassborow here in the city. His experience in writing for radio, film, television and stage was invaluable.

The work began in earnest in the spring of 2007, calling a meeting on 21 March of all interested parties, from the city, county, education, schools, churches, choirs, musicians etc. At that stage we had a vision and logo, designed by Sophie Hacker, and a great deal of commitment. By the time of the launch service in the Cathedral on 30 September we had most of the script, some of the directors and we were conscious of huge mountains to climb. Originally we had

The Passion in Winchester by Judy Strafford

envisaged being inside the Cathedral for the finale, but it became clear early on that the mounting interest meant the audience numbers would be too great. Instead, Jesus would have to be crucified on the balcony of the west face of the Cathedral, overlooking the city.

We found ourselves engaged in all kinds of new experiences, such as writing a detailed (the final copy ran to just under 100 pages) Event Management Plan, longer even than the script. There were almost more volunteers than we could cope with. So many people wanted to sing (there were no less than eight choirs involved already) that Sarah Morgan of the Winchester Community Choir kindly agreed to form a new Passion Chorale of 80 voices. The distribution of news about the Passion was vital and we combined praying and distribution with a process devised by Juli Wills of 'Prayer and Packing': praying for the Passion in the chapel of the United Church and then preparing 6,000 leaflets into bundles of information for distribution to churches and groups across the region.

As well as a logo we needed an image to promote the Passion across the city and beyond. Two local artists were commissioned and we decided to use the painting by Judy Strafford as the main image for all publicity leading up to the event. Her composition bringing all the main buildings into one location with Jesus carrying a cross beam remains captivating. Its fresh image brought immediate recognition and carried all the publicity.

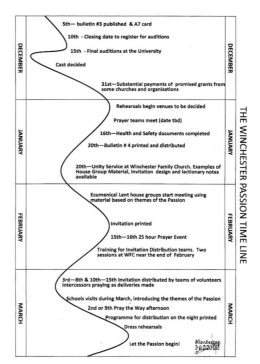

		THE WINCHESTER PASSION TIME LINE
DECEMBER	5th— bulletin #3 published & A7 card	**DECEMBER**
	10th - Closing date to register for auditions	
	15th - Final auditions at the University	
	Cast decided	
	31st—Substantial payments of promised grants from some churches and organisations	
JANUARY	Rehearsals begin venues to be decided	**JANUARY**
	Prayer teams meet (date tbd)	
	16th—Health and Safety documents completed	
	20th—Bulletin # 4 printed and distributed	
	20th—Unity Service at Winchester Family Church. Examples of House Group Material, Invitation design and lectionary notes available	
FEBRUARY	Ecumenical Lent house groups start meeting using material based on themes of the Passion	**FEBRUARY**
	Invitation printed	
	15th—16th 25 hour Prayer Event	
	Training for Invitation Distribution teams. Two sessions at WFC near the end of February	
MARCH	3rd—8th & 10th—15th Invitation distributed by teams of volunteers intercessors praying as deliveries made	**MARCH**
	Schools visits during March, introducing the themes of the Passion	
	2nd or 9th Pray the Way afternoon	
	Programme for distribution on the night printed	
	Dress rehearsals	
	Let the Passion begin!	*Winchester PASSION*

Part of the Time Line Planning

The Winchester Passion logo by Sophie Hacker

A project such as this costs a bob or two(!) and though several trusts and businesses kindly gave us grants, the churches and generous individual donors shouldered the bulk of the financial burden. Mention has to be made of the team of wonderful Producers without which it simply would not have happened. Most are busy clergy but their churches gave them the space to undertake this work. Ewen Huffman (Winchester Baptist Church) who drove the technical side, David Williams (Christ Church, C of E) who built huge teams for the management of the various sites and traffic flow, and Roly Riem (Cathedral) whose creative ministry was so important. Of course crucial to their group was Philip Glassborow. Also from Christ Church came Yvonne Secker who organised a whole team of seamstresses to provide the costume wardrobe, and Jeremy Davies who held both faith and the budget. We were wonderfully resourced by Juli Wills as Project

The lighting tower

Manager (who also kept our noses to the detail of it all), and Naomi Honey on admin support, both working for the United Church. It was my privilege to lead this team and to co-ordinate the project. Preparing this publication has given me the joy of reliving that remarkable event.

As the autumn proceeded, exhaustive local auditions were held in various locations and gradually the key characters were identified – with one exception. Who would play the part of Jesus? By this time, BBC Radio Solent were on board and Tim Daykin on his Sunday morning programme joined us in the 'search for Jesus' which was, curiously enough, at its height during epiphany, the time we celebrate the wise men looking for Jesus. Eventually we discovered Israel Oyelumade and it is difficult now to

Early walk-through of city streets with four reverend gentlemen: Howard Mellor, Roly Riem, Jeremy Davies (visiting from Salisbury to give advice) and David Williams.

think of anyone better for the part. His professional ability as an actor is beyond question and his firm personal faith in God shone out from him. Indeed, in the rehearsals Israel's presence immediately lifted the quality of acting and commitment.

The Winchester Passion was a modern retelling of the betrayal, death and resurrection of Jesus. At 6pm Jesus and his followers entered the city at Oram's Arbour where a festival was taking place under the watchful eye of the Roman army. In the aftermath Barabbas was arrested after a fierce battle with well-equipped soldiers. At the Great Hall Jesus met with his disciples for the Last Supper, and Judas decided to betray him. Leaving the supper, Jesus went to Gethsemane and was then arrested and brought before a scandalized Caiaphas, a reluctant Pilate and an incredulous Herod outside the Law Courts. Condemned, Jesus carried his cross down the High Street, past the Buttercross before being crucified with two criminals outside the Cathedral. Dead, he was taken down from the cross and buried. Then the miraculous resurrection took place, with recognition by Mary Magdalene. Jesus walked out of the Cathedral into the crowded city promising always to be with us, until the very end of time.

At the end of Radio Solent's live three-hour broadcast, the commentators in the studio summed up the event as one which had 'reclaimed Easter for Christianity.' It clearly touched many lives. People wrote, phoned and stopped us in the street to explain what they 'saw' and how the Passion had affected them. For all of that, especially the privilege of being part of this event, Praise be to God for His blessing and grace.

Howard Mellor

G. Howard Mellor
Minister of the United Church, Winchester
and Chair of the Passion

Doug Bennett (left) with some of the lighting team

Nicodemus challenges Jesus: 'Who do you think you are?'

On Oram's Arbour, Jesus enters the Holy City

Jairus and his daughter defend Jesus to the Pharisee leaders

The Passover festival in Jerusalem, reconceived as a village fete in Winchester

Barabbas and his men are arrested by the Roman soldiers

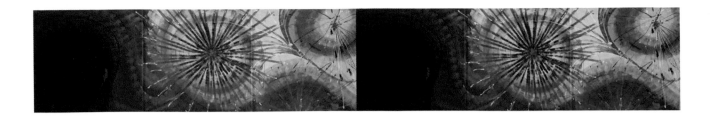

1   A Passion for Winchester

Philip Glassborow

Artistic Director and writer of *The Winchester Passion, 2008*

PHILIP GLASSBOROW

Philip Glassborow is a writer and director working in theatre, television, film and radio. His many credits include award-winning dramatisations and documentaries, features and original dramas. Recent broadcasts for BBC Radio 4 include Christopher Himself *starring David Suchet and Bernard Cribbins,* The Gorey Details, *and a programme about Maurice Sendak which he also presented. His radio dramatisation of* Peter Pan *(starring Toyah Willcox, Ron Moody and June Whitfield) was nominated for a Writers' Guild Award and is available on CD from BBC Audio. Philip has also written two musicals for the Watermill Theatre in Newbury.*

It's all Howard's fault. He's the chap who had the bright idea. Having seen the BBC's Manchester Passion on television, he said, 'Well, if there can be a Manchester Passion, why not a *Winchester* Passion?'

The big question was – could we find a distinctive way of telling the story for our own city and for our own time, 2008? The BBC had produced a big event for TV using the pop songs of 21st century Manchester singer-songwriters. The BBC had resources, lights and cameras, resources, personnel and expertise, resources, professional musicians, and singers, and actors like Keith Allen, and – yes – resources!

By contrast, we had five loaves and two small fish…

But there are many ways to tell a story. Closer to home, there was 'The Way of the Cross' at Salisbury for inspiration. There was fine work at Wintershall in Surrey. And of course, there was Bach's glorious *Matthew Passion*. While, for contrast, there was also Mel Gibson's *The Passion of the Christ* – a movie version of the story for the Tarantino generation, with an abundant transfusion of blood…

Not to mention twenty centuries of artistic masterpieces inspired by this extraordinary theme. Drawings, paintings, statues, carvings and representations in all media of the suffering and death and resurrection of Jesus. From ancient and medieval works, to the Old Masters, to Salvador Dali, Stanley Spencer and beyond.

So, how could we make our production a *Winchester* Passion? How could we recapture the shocking rawness of an old, familiar story in visuals and iconography that would have meaning for a contemporary audience?

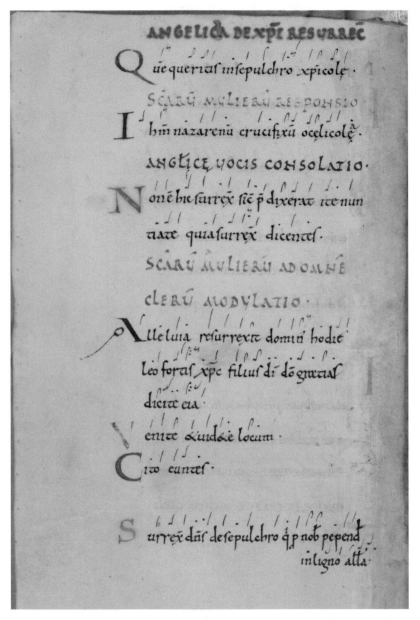

The Quem Quaeritis page from The Winchester Troper in the Parker Library.
Reproduced by permission of the Master and Fellows of Corpus Christi College, Cambridge

But the Cross is – literally – crucial to the Passion. It has to be a barbaric, hideous, excruciating death; a grotesque public humiliation; an obscenity to the Jews; a stumbling block to the Gentiles; the ultimate symbol of suffering. We could modernize the crown of thorns as a wreath of barbed wire. But the Cross must stand.

Back to our city, and Winchester's literary heritage also proved to be fruitful and felicitous. We found no medieval tradition here of Mystery Plays, as there is in cities like York or Chester. So there were no existing local Passion texts to inspire us. Except for one extraordinary document: *The Winchester Troper.*

Centuries before the medieval era, back in the mists of Anglo-Saxon history, part of the Passion story was re-enacted each year in church during Easter worship. (This dialogue marks the very dawning of drama on our shores. How exciting to think that theatre in Britain began as part of Christian liturgy!)

A priest, in the role of an angel, called out *'Quem quaeritis in sepulchro, Christicolae?'* (Who do you seek in the sepulchre, you followers of Jesus?) – and others, speaking for the women at the tomb, replied *'Jesum Nazarenum crucifixium, o caelicolae'* (We seek Jesus of Nazareth who was crucified, you celestial angels). It so happens that the very earliest written record of this dialogue is preserved in a tiny volume known as *The Winchester Troper.* This precious little book, with ancient writing still clear and bright on its vellum pages, dates from around 970 AD. It predates even our venerable cathedral, having been used in the previous building on the same

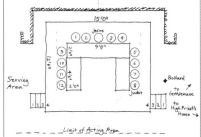

We originally planned to stage the Last Supper scene inside Winchester's Great Hall. Instead of seating Jesus and the disciples at a long straight table – as in Leonardo da Vinci's painting – we envisaged them at a round table. This would also have a particular site-specific resonance, as the fabled Arthurian 'Round Table' is displayed inside the Great Hall. I was delighted to discover this drawing in an old children's book, showing the scene just as I had imagined it.

However, almost a thousand people attended the service in September 2007 at Winchester Cathedral to launch the Passion initiative. Thus, it was estimated that the audience for the actual Good Friday event itself might be in the region of 3,000 or even more. As a result, we could no longer plan on using any interiors: even the Cathedral could only contain an audience of 2,000. So the Last Supper was, instead, staged in a courtyard outside the Great Hall, where the location and sightlines required a different design for the table.

25

site, Old Minster. This unique survivor appears to have been the choir-master's own copy (the cantor's name, we believe, was Wulfstan), and contains music notation in an extremely old form. Anglo-Saxon music was written in 'neumes' which until very recently were thought to be undecipherable. However, just in the last few years, musicologists have found a way to recreate the melodies, harmonies and rhythms from these impossibly ancient scores.

So – here was a dramatic Passion dialogue, enacted within an Easter service, and first written down here in our very own city! We were delighted to be able to use a brief section of Latin within our script.

The next literary and historic link was thanks to good King Alfred, a wise and reverend ruler of Wessex. Alfred's wife Ealswitha was benefactress of the Nunnaminster in Winchester, where Anglo-Saxon nuns wrote vivid and poetic prayers of the passion, which David Scott explores in his article within these pages. Also here in that epoch, a book was compiled of patterns of worship, and this volume (*Regularis Concordia*) includes the haunting prayer that we borrowed from history to stand at the heart of our new Winchester Passion:

Lord Jesus Christ, I adore thee ascending the Cross.

(The full text is printed on page 61 in David Scott's article.) This beautiful prayer was already hallowed by time when it was included within the Benedictine Easter ritual at the Synod of Winchester in 970 AD – it dates back even earlier, to around 750 AD! Imagine our delight when Sir John Tavener agreed to set this timeless prayer to music. It was a great privilege to feature the world premiere of a new choral composition by Sir John Tavener at the climax of our event.

Sir John Tavener

In the limited space remaining, may I discuss the way I explored two challenges as a playwright? The Passion is indeed 'The Greatest Story Ever Told' and is full of drama and spectacle. Some of the events, such as the entry to Jerusalem, are on a grand scale. Others, like the washing of the disciples' feet by Jesus, are intimate, private, domestic. Indeed, all the ingredients of theatre are here: trial scenes, betrayals, conspiracies, arrests, executions, cataclysmic miracles. But nevertheless, the overall story needs to be given a dramatic shape.

If that sounds like sacrilege – surely the Bible needs no embellishment? – then I'll offer an example of 'shaping' in our treatment of the character, Barabbas. In the Gospels, we only encounter him at the climactic trial scene near the end of the Passion accounts. However, for dramatic structure, it seemed important that we should meet him before then and establish some of his 'back story'.

Accordingly, we followed the tradition that Barabbas was a Jewish zealot who was fighting back against the tyranny of Rome. A murderer, yes, but a warrior too, motivated by religious fervour. To the devout Jews, he would have been seen as a freedom fighter. While to the Romans, he was a terrorist.

How better to introduce this character than by staging his arrest and capture by the Roman army? This included an action-packed fight scene directed by Neil Simpson, an expert in physical theatre. The drama served to underscore the seething political tensions in Jerusalem at Passover time. Furthermore, we could establish other characters at the same time: the two 'thieves' who would later be crucified on either side of Jesus. They could be members of Barabbas' guerilla army, which is why they would be sentenced to such a hideous and public execution.

Adding to the drama of the scene, we imagined that Barabbas actually wanted the glory of martyrdom (with resonances here of a modern-day suicide bomber). So being set free was, for him, an ironical tragedy of his own. As Jesus was led away for crucifixion, Barabbas called out, 'No! It should have been me! It should have been me!'

The second example of dramatic structuring – or dramatic licence, perhaps – is the question of Judas. Surely one of the great enigmas of all time is: why did this disciple betray his friend and Master? There are countless theories, ranging from the idea that Judas was disappointed in Jesus as a revolutionary leader, and was trying to provoke some kind of political crisis, to the simple economic: 'He did it for the money.'

We always, as human beings, want to know the reasons and motivations for people's actions. Why did she say that? What made him do that? Yet in 'real life', we can't always discern why people act the way they do. (And in a play like *Othello*, Shakespeare does not actually provide any cut-and-dried reasons for Iago's jealousy and treachery. 'Stuff just happens,' as the Bard never actually said.)

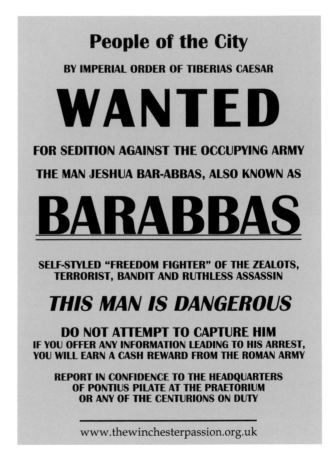

People of the City

BY IMPERIAL ORDER OF TIBERIAS CAESAR

WANTED

FOR SEDITION AGAINST THE OCCUPYING ARMY

THE MAN JESHUA BAR-ABBAS, ALSO KNOWN AS

BARABBAS

SELF-STYLED "FREEDOM FIGHTER" OF THE ZEALOTS, TERRORIST, BANDIT AND RUTHLESS ASSASSIN

THIS MAN IS DANGEROUS

DO NOT ATTEMPT TO CAPTURE HIM
IF YOU OFFER ANY INFORMATION LEADING TO HIS ARREST, YOU WILL EARN A CASH REWARD FROM THE ROMAN ARMY

REPORT IN CONFIDENCE TO THE HEADQUARTERS OF PONTIUS PILATE AT THE PRAETORIUM OR ANY OF THE CENTURIONS ON DUTY

www.thewinchesterpassion.org.uk

One of the notices fly-posted around the city in the run-up to the event

We have several clues to Judas's actions in the Gospels. John 12:6 even asserts baldly that Judas had his hand in the till: 'This he said, not that he cared for the poor, but because he was a thief, and had the bag, and what was put therein.'

Luke 22:3 is equally uncompromising: 'Then entered Satan into Judas surnamed Iscariot, being of the number of the twelve.' But how could a concept like that be represented in the theatre? How would Satan twist his mind? Desire for money? Pride? Fear?

In my first draft, we saw Judas being persuaded to betray Jesus immediately after the arrest of Barabbas. So the audience could infer that Judas was partly frightened into his betrayal. He had just seen for himself, yet again, the ruthlessness of the Romans in action. He was therefore easy game for the Captain of the Temple Guard, who could play on his instinct for self-preservation.

Then we changed the sequence of events to harmonise with Matthew and Mark, so the betrayal scene followed Judas being rebuked by Jesus. (You'll recall that Judas had protested at the waste of money when Jesus was anointed with precious oil of nard.) This now suggested anger as a further layer of motivation – perhaps indeed the final straw. Judas was hurt and angry at this rebuke, as well as being frightened of arrest by the Romans, and tempted by the money on offer from the priests.

Dear reader, I wish we had space to share some of the other challenges we grappled with!

How Dr Cecily O'Neill triumphantly solved the problem of representing the angels at the tomb for the 21st century: a young man in white, according to Mark; two men in shining garments, as Luke describes them; but did you realise that they also *danced*, with stately grace and mystical authority?

How we portrayed a final temptation of Christ, as he suffered on the cross…

How Geoffrey Burnaby managed to stage the washing of the feet – with all twelve disciples – on a tiny platform which then transformed effortlessly into the scene of the Last Supper…

How John Rynne's off-the-cuff idea turned into a huge scaffolding stage for the crucifixion and resurrection scenes, being constructed high above the west doorway of Winchester Cathedral…

And those were just a few of the challenges for the *drama* group! There were also splendid teams building the staging and designing the lighting and making the costumes and arranging a phalanx of radio microphones and beaming television pictures from location to location, where they could be shown on vast screens towering over the action.

Suffice it to say that the Good Lord was gracious enough to accept our five loaves and two small fish. He worked a miracle that night for the hundreds who took part in, and the thousands who experienced, The Winchester Passion 2008.

The audience follows Jesus down to the Great Hall

The disciples with Jesus

*Mary of Magdala anoints Jesus
with precious oil of nard*

Judas meets the Captain of the Temple Guard

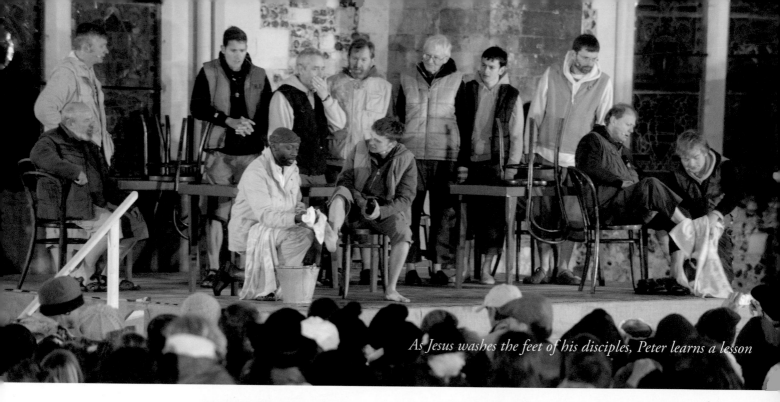

As Jesus washes the feet of his disciples, Peter learns a lesson

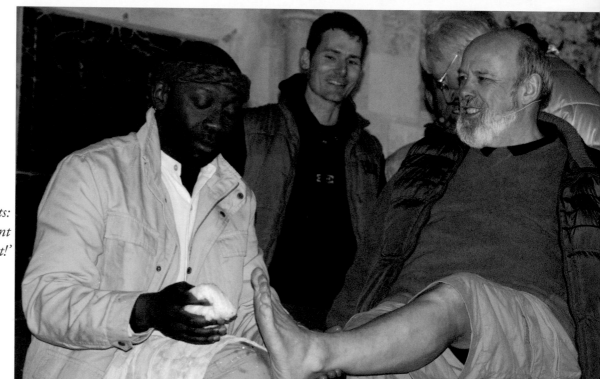

Matthew Levi protests: 'Oh no, you don't want my feet!'

32

2   **People of the Passion**

Roland Riem
Canon Pastor & Missioner

ROLY REIM

Roland Riem is a Canon at Winchester Cathedral with responsibilities for education, visitor welcome and for certain mission and ecumenical partnerships. He enjoys film and drama and is married to the artist responsible for the Passion logo, Sophie Hacker. He was previously involved in theological education in Salisbury and has also served as a university chaplain.

I was delighted to produce a series of six character studies for the Passion programme . The Passion story teems with human interest. People are constantly bouncing off the Mystery in their midst, their expectations, histories and ambitions all contributing to a rich and absorbing drama. I saw this project as a way of helping people to probe various reactions which Jesus could provoke, so allowing readers to form their own judgements about Jesus.

Freedom to respond to Jesus in one's own unique way lies at the heart of the gospel. We have Herodias and Mary Magdalene, both women, one seeing Christ as a threat, the other as the very hinge and pivot of her own existence. The men are provoked in various ways. Barabbas shows irony and cynicism, but not the fear of Herodias; Peter's brokenness and longing mirrors Mary's, but his remains unfulfilled; Joseph of Arimathea gives us a sense of common decency and compromised admiration entirely absent from Barabbas' vision of justice. Lastly we have the angels pondering on the benefits of being human from the outside-in, giving a detached but kindly judgement on our fleshly perspective on resurrection.

I hope to evoke rather than criticise how people can be: all responses are possible; some are closer to the Truth than others. But with Christ the Truth is always closer than expected, which is what makes each of these studies an invitation to make the next move towards Him. He stands with us in all our seeking.

Herodias

Clare Carson

Technically, I admit, the Law forbids marriage to the brother of a living husband; but who in our day takes these traditions seriously? Was I to heed the cries of a madman, someone who roamed the wilderness crying that our nation's exile had ended? Unlikely, I feel. The baptiser John was an embarrassment. He deserved his fate at my husband's hand, even if my dear Salome's charms were needed.

The only strategy worth pursuing in this sorry world, I have found, is to reach for as much influence and wealth as one can muster. A woman must marry carefully, and if a brighter prospect appears, abandon the folly of former ways and re-marry; and so much better if a brother is available.

Rumours spread of John's return (such tales always amuse the masses), but who could mistake the Baptist for this 'Christ', an altogether saner fellow, not one to bleat about my domestic affairs? My husband, though, should have shown more dignity: I watched him prodding at his chest, taunting and troubled. It worried me.

I'd thought my Herod strong enough to climb high, with our shared family name – the prince and his queen. But looking at him now, I begin to fear. John's words, for all their fury, caused us less damage than this man's deeds.

Our people must not rise above their station. They must not catch the whiff of hope in the air. We thrive best when others live in resignation.

Simon Peter

I love him to death, actually. Well, now I can say that honestly, I think. You can never be sure till it comes to the crunch. And looking back I can see he was testing me long before we got that far. Even calling me 'Rock' was a challenge. What a name to live up to, especially for someone as impetuous as me.

But the trouble with Jesus was that he was unpredictable. Even a meal could be a lesson. What would you do if your leader suddenly got up from the table and started doing a slave's work? Washing our feet – I couldn't make head nor tail of it. But there he was starting with mine, saying he had to do it. I tried to duck out, but there was no escape. I still look at my feet and wonder why he wanted to bend so low.

Rita caught me off guard, too, outside the High Priest's house. I still cringe at my betrayal. God knows, I was only trying to protect myself. I got away as fast as my feet would carry me – my dirty feet, doing exactly the opposite to what I'd hoped and promised.

Since then I've had plenty of time for tears, thinking of the place where our paths uncrossed. But I hope against hope that he'll give me one last chance to follow in his steps – however, wherever he wills – and this time right to the end.

Michael Alborough

35

Barabbas

Marcus Chapman

Justice is what I was after – justice for the people. No wonder they loved me. No wonder they chose me not Jesus, the so-called Messiah.

I guess the priests set the whole thing up, getting a popular freedom fighter to stand against a failed deliverer.

He'd had his chance, mind. So many fine words, some pretty miracles – he even healed the poor and stood them on their feet. But where was the fire? Where was the force to back up the vision? No wonder his followers deserted him.

In my world men fight for what they hold dear – they don't mince words with religious authorities. What's theology got to do with crushing the enemy!

I'm told he called God 'Abba' – Father. That's the most he and I have in common. They call me Barabbas, son of Abba, and I'm proud to come from a long line of fighters. We all know that God sides with his martyrs.

Ironic that Jesus ended up on the block, when I was the one prepared to stick my neck out, to die in a blaze of glory. But he took the rap. Meek as a lamb, he went. No cursing, no struggle. No one's going to get too excited about that, least of all me – a failed martyr now, I suppose. Luck of the gods, I call it.

At least, Jesus, you managed to save this one victim from death. You might have liked that – not that you ever intended it!

Mary of Magdala

Now I find I live stretched between two equal memories of him, at once both sad and joyful. To this day I don't know what propelled me to where he was staying, and why I found myself pouring my one great extravagance onto his feet – the bottle of perfume broken, the scent pervasive, my hair tumbling about his toes – a moment of sheer abandon, till he converted it. My actions had a meaning, he said, beyond generosity and an urge to comfort him – an anointing for his death. I shuddered at the thought of what I'd done.

As we women stood near the cross watching his agony, I remembered that ritual undertaken inadvertently. His death had really come about, as he had prophesied. But had my perfume laid a scent for his pursuers?

The second memory is of rising early, to be close again to his body and to fetch the necessary spices. This time sadness first: who had taken him away, denying me my last kind touch and tender ministry? Again, he converted the moment, coming to me like a gardener to plant a seed of hope. Mary! Jesus said, and I knew it was he.

He told me not to cling to him as he had not yet returned home to his Father. So I let him go, my joyful heart in abandon. My Lord had made me a witness, not of his death but of life beyond the grave, which no one could ever destroy.

Polly Perry

Angels

Tim and Matt Honey

What, you may wonder, were we doing outside the tomb? Seldom do we step down from the heavenly courts to show ourselves – you find us too unsettling to be routinely met, even in human form. But when the tide of history turns we must make our mark and herald the news with which we're charged.

You humans are so apt to go astray. Even those whose great love holds them to the cross and grave end up divorced from truth, weeping at loss or wandering aimless in dismay. Yet Christ is alive, freed from the rot and stench of death.

We spirits will never truly comprehend what it is like to raise up flesh, but we do know well the realm into which Christ has passed. It is our familiar place; so we ask, 'Who do you seek in the sepulchre, you followers of Jesus?'

We are patient tutors. When we speak, we tell you to be unafraid, not simply of our sudden appearing but of the vastness of things unseen to which we point, which make you quake at their immensity. How hard it is to look beyond dead ends, to see the leaps and vaults of God; but that is why we're sent.

The one you seek is not here, trapped by time or stone. We judge with love this fruitless search of yours, and yet bring grace, because beyond what you can grasp is his body glorified, and offered to make you whole.

Joseph of Arimathea

Unless you've actually sat on the Tribunal, you can't know how hard it is to balance the facts of a case. I'm known as a moderate member, sometimes too keen to see every side of an argument, but generally held in respect, not just for my wealth, a sign of blessing from God, but because I understand due process. Without the keeping to Law how would we honour the most High God and keep peace in the land? Without his favour we are lost.

It is simply a legal fact that witnesses are needed to condemn a man. There are checks and balances in our system, and a two-thirds majority required. We are not animals. But blasphemy, real or supposed, helps nobody's cause. I am not an unreasonable man, and I could not myself vote for his death. Besides, I'd heard strange words like this from him before, words riddled with truth.

A wealthy man may not be able to change the world, but he has means to make redress. Somewhere in my bones I knew he deserved better than he got, that I could offer mercy to this man beaten up on his way … that Samaritan parable of his was always my favourite. The keeper of Law who passed by on the other side, that man will not be me.

So, Jesus, have my grave. Even though I failed to heal your wounds, here in my gift is lodging where you can stay. I wish you rest.

Philip Tutt-Leppard

3   Through the eyes of 'Jesus'

Israel Oyelumade

ISRAEL OYELUMADE

Israel Oyelumade is a graduate of RADA and has worked extensively in theatre, television, film and radio He is also an Ambassador for the Prince's Trust and a founder/director of InService Productions. He has played many parts on stage and screen but has never faced a more important and challenging role. He said 'Jesus is God in a man's body and that's all I can really play him as. It's a role that can't be any bigger.'

On a cold mid-December evening in 2007, my phone rang. Unaware of what was to follow I answered in my usual relaxed manner.

By the time I had ended my call from producer/director Philip Glassborow, I had accepted the invitation to portray the greatest man to ever walk the earth … Jesus Christ, the Son of God.

From that time onwards the one thought that consumed me was how to demonstrate and become the very essence of Christ himself. Being a professional actor is one thing, however when coupled with my faith as a 'born again' Christian, it made this project very unique indeed.

What was it about Jesus that drew his disciples and thousands of followers to him …? I was about to embark on a journey that would change me to the core of my being.

As my wife and son helped me move into our momentary home in Winchester, a sense of foreboding began to swell on the inside of me. The scale of the task that lay ahead was beginning to be realised – 'What was I thinking?'; 'Had I heard God right?'; 'Should I have taken another project?' However, my saving grace was the simple fact that I had sensed through God, that a particular project was about to come to me and I was to wait until that happened. Fortunately, I only had to turn down two other possibilities before the December phone call, thus preventing my agent from calling me crazy.

As I look back on what turned out to be an historic occasion for both Winchester and country, I am still awestruck at what took place on that cold damp evening of 21 March 2008, and what caused 12,000 people to stand in stunned silence for some three hours whilst braving the natural elements.

'Being' Jesus was, and I've little doubt will remain, one of the highest points in my acting career. I realised that Jesus was the quintessential leading man; he led by example in speech and in deed.

This caused me to attempt to mirror him in rehearsals, meetings, in fact at every given opportunity, and as I did this an interesting thing started to happen … As we got further into rehearsals my affection towards my fellow cast members started to grow very strong and I noticed that as I talked to and watched each actor/disciple it was as if I felt that I began to know more about them than they knew about themselves. In return, the way I was being treated was with a level of respect and in some cases, dare I say it, reverence and honour unlike any project I had worked on before.

So as we acted out scene after scene I began to understand the patience Jesus had with his disciples. He knew he was en route to somewhere else, a place they could not comprehend.

I took genuine pity on my fellow actors as I could see what was coming: they were about to be part of a city-stopping event that would call for their nerves to hold fast and wait.

As we got closer to the historic day all I could do was pray and read and re-read the various points of view of the disciples of Jesus.

On the morning of the Winchester Passion itself I felt very fragile. It's a feeling I have come to know when God is doing something in my heart. He was answering my prayers for what I knew I needed to happen within me to be able to let my offering of Christ live and breathe. My wife Catharine took care of all our family and guests arriving in their various states of excitement, thus enabling me to set my mind on the cross.

All of a sudden it was 4.30pm and the entire cast were getting dressed and going to the various starting points. Oram's Arbour was ablaze with army trucks, colour and music; donkeys were ready, the BBC Radio Solent in full swing with their live broadcast, TV cameras in all their filming positions. So, 64 radio mikes later, on the stroke of 6pm, my journey began.

The first sight of the crowds was overwhelming. Into this small city 12,000 people from all over the country converged towards its four main landmarks. Oh, and I forgot to say, imagine that all of them are looking at you, the honoured guest that all had come to see. It was scary, exhilarating and humbling.

As we left Orams Arbour to go towards the law courts to continue the next scenes, I truly understood how amazingly difficult it must have been for Jesus – a constant sea of people everywhere he turned, streets crammed with people, thrusting their children in front of him, fortunately for him there were no digital camcorders, for me…no such luck! It got so charged with expectancy I could hardly breathe, how on earth would I get through the crowd? I would have to teach en route to my next encounter, just as Jesus did.

By now I was getting cold, still damp from the 6pm downpour. My disciples and I were edging towards 'the washing of the feet,' blessing, touching, intensely focussed as I made my way through. When the oil of spikenard was poured lovingly over my feet I stopped acting and just 'became'. Everything I was now doing was centred in Christ, He was now in the driving seat and I was a willing passenger. I could sense my eyes burning with His light, His fire, He had me right where He wanted me – after all, this event was all about Him.

As the trial scenes took place, my body trembling beyond my control, I stood under the blanket of a star-glistened night and knew God was watching. I felt His embracing presence holding me, willing me to rest in Him.

My head crowned with thorns, blood dripping from my scalp … I can only imagine what Jesus went through, I willed myself to feel the numbness of my feet in my open sandals as the cross beam was strapped across my back. How does a man walk to his death whipped and beaten within an inch of his life? And yet still carry a presence and dignity that is not of this world?

What God can prevent in his power he will allow in his wisdom.

I walked the 'Via Dolorosa' behind a thief and a bandit, yet I did not see them; people mocking me, crying in sympathy for me, emptying pubs and restaurants, not knowing what to do or say – they just stood, some in shock, some in wonder, yet still I did not see them. My journey was becoming increasingly personal, my internal dialogue evermore earnest. I stumbled at the Buttercross and as I looked into the eyes that wiped my brow I saw mercy. Every good and pure act was a strengthening of my resolve, yet the ultimate act of mercy and love was His life for us.

I am now walking alone towards Winchester Cathedral past the huge TV screens, all I can hear is the faint mumble of a the BBC Radio Solent live broadcast reporting my every move.

My steps get heavier and my body starts to cramp as the music underscores every breath and sigh. Finally I reach my destination. Within the confines of that sacred monument there is only time enough for a costume change, just then, I break! It's too much to bear. I start to grieve, so deep is the well from whence it came, it cannot be contained. I make my way up the stairs still sobbing, to the Crucifixion.

No truer words were ever spoken than when Jesus was on the cross. As I looked out over the sea of people looking up towards the west face of the cathedral balcony I could see the moon giving us its full attention, my scream of pain that rang out over the cathedral grounds hovered and reverberated as if to celebrate Christ's last words, 'It is finished.' The moon then moved behind the cloud, I wonder, was my Father in heaven taking care of the special effects?

From here on in it was joy unspeakable, dressed in white and gold, resurrected! I had exchanged my thorns for a crown! Life came back into my being as I pushed open the central cathedral doors emblazoned in the powerful shafts of light (my resurrection glory). I could see another journey just beginning. And as I surveyed my wondrous cross I truly understood its victory message…that Christ was going to his Father and my Father for one day soon, we will all be together!

Soon Lord, soon.

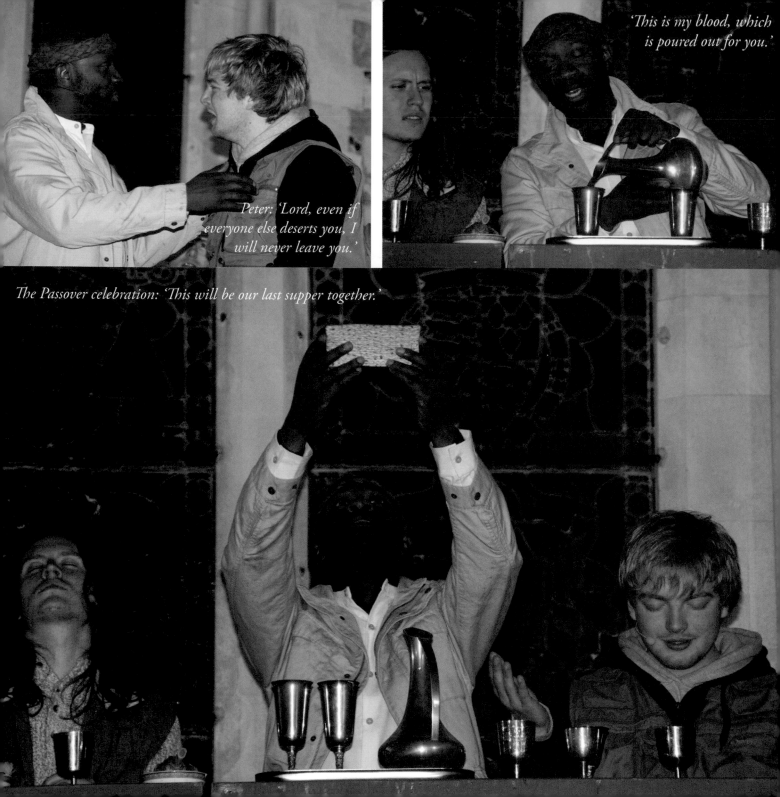

'This is my blood, which is poured out for you.'

Peter: 'Lord, even if everyone else deserts you, I will never leave you.'

The Passover celebration: 'This will be our last supper together.'

GETHSEMANE BLUES

Jesus went out in the garden to pray:
He said, Father, tell me Father, does it have to be this way?
But his Father didn't answer. His Father didn't answer.

He prayed in the garden of Gethsemane,
Can't someone else do this – or does it have to be me?
But his Father didn't answer. His Father didn't answer.

Jesus dropped down to his knees and prayed,
He said, Father, help me Father, cause I feel so afraid.
But his Father didn't answer. His Father didn't answer.

Jesus prayed so hard there was sweat on his head,
He said, Father, please send somebody else instead…
But his Father didn't answer. His Father didn't answer.

Jesus lay down in the dirt on his face
And prayed, Some other time, Father, some other place?
But his Father didn't answer. His Father didn't answer.

Jesus said, Father, I can face the pain,
But what if I never see you again?
But his Father didn't answer. His Father didn't answer.

Why was there no answer? He already knew the answer.
No one else could do it. Who else could go through it?
It had to be this way, and it had to be today.

So Jesus stood up in Gethsemane,
And said, All right, Father, if it has to be me,
So be it. So be it.

And his Father answered – just one word.
The saddest 'Amen' you ever heard
Was the Father's answer.

'When you're far from home...'

4   Staging the Winchester Passion

Cecily O'Neill

CECILY O'NEILL

Dr Cecily O'Neill is an international authority on Process Drama and the arts in education. She works with students, teachers, directors and actors throughout the world, leading drama workshops, speaking at conferences and carrying out research. She is an Associate Artist with the Unicorn Theatre in London, and a visiting lecturer and examiner at universities in the UK, the USA and Australia. Dr O'Neill is the author and editor of several influential books on drama.

When I first became involved in the Winchester Passion, I realised that as it would be taking take place on Good Friday, the evening of 21 March – the earliest Easter for years – it was quite likely to be both wet and cold. The writer Philip Glassborow had placed the action in a variety of stunning locations – from the windswept Oram's Arbour through the narrow streets of the city. I read through the script until I got to the Resurrection. At that point in the planning it was hoped that this final segment might take place inside the Cathedral. So, because I thought it would take place indoors, I offered to direct that part. But I soon found out that it would be impractical to try to stage a performance inside the Cathedral on the busiest weekend of the church's calendar as well as being impossible to move the audience indoors. We'd anticipated that perhaps a few thousand people might attend the performance. In the event it's been calculated that it was witnessed by about 12,000 people.

Next I discovered that I would be responsible for directing the Crucifixion as well as the Resurrection, both central events in Christian belief, which would be staged on the balcony above the West Door of the Cathedral. I was excited about the possibilities this location offered, but daunted by the challenges we would have to face. The balcony, which is more of an architectural decoration than a real platform, is high above the West Door of the Cathedral – 30 steps up a narrow winding stair. A platform would have to be built so that the actors would be visible above the parapet. What would it be like to work at such a height? Would any of the actors suffer from vertigo? Could we make it safe to move about picture of angels wearing long tunics but I also found one dressed in trousers and a shirt and rather bright colours in a depiction of a Bible story. In the performance our angels were dressed in white cheesecloth tops and white jeans. We developed a sequence of movements based on the gestures of the angels in these pictures, whether they were messengers, guardians, musicians or warriors. Even within the limitations of the high narrow platform on which they stood, their movements became a solemn dance. In his search for weapons for the soldiery, Philip had discovered a pair of long lances which became a crucial addition to the gestures of the angels. They helped the boys to convey the necessary power and authority of God's messengers and certainly compensated for their lack of wings.

For everybody involved in the event the months of preparation for the Winchester Passion were a time of intense reflection and research. I found that the study of Christian iconography, particularly of the actual crucifixion itself, was crucial to exploring the kinds of images it might be possible to present. In the imagery of the Passion, the gaze of Christ is very important. He gazes at Judas who will betray him and at Peter who has denied him – 'And the Lord turned and looked upon Peter, and Peter went out and wept bitterly'. Because of the scale of the production and the distances involved, these details may not have been apparent to many of the spectators. But those of us working on the balcony above the West Door were very aware of the power and presence that Israel Oyelumade, the only professional actor in the cast, managed to convey. He quelled the ribald soldier with a glance and in his eyes was the clear recognition of the penitence of the thief as well as the promise of redemption.

I was reminded of what Samuel Beckett said: 'Don't presume. Remember that one of the thieves was damned. Don't despair. Remember one of the thieves was saved.' That idea has stayed very strongly with me. Philip, in giving the Winchester Passion a contemporary edge, re-imagined the thieves as terrorists. In rehearsal one night, I told the bad terrorist, who was quite a young actor, that if Jesus hadn't been dying from crucifixion he'd be dying from the evil looks the actor had been giving him. As we rehearsed on the balcony tourists and passers-by were electrified by

the same actor shrieking 'Death to the Romans!' as he was fastened to the cross.

How would we manage to crucify three actors without harming them? Clearly we couldn't attempt anything naturalistic! It was very important that the 'bodies' should be removed from the crosses without injury, and a helpful member of the fire-brigade demonstrated safe and effective ways of carrying the actors from the stage. Keeping everything as simple as possible, scaffolding poles were used as uprights and the soldiers fastened the actors to crossbeams with red streamers. Even when we were not rehearsing, these stark, empty crosses silhouetted against the great West Window of the Cathedral made a powerful statement.

Once the platform and scaffolding were in place we began rehearsals on the Cathedral balcony. Our greatest challenge was the cold. Most of the actors worked during the day, so we had to rehearse in the last glimmers of daylight. Everyone wore as many layers of clothing as possible, and in spite of constant hot drinks provided by a wonderful volunteer, we were soon blue with cold. Israel was bravely determined that he would strip to the waist for the actual Crucifixion on Good Friday, but in the event the cold defeated him and he kept his shirt on.

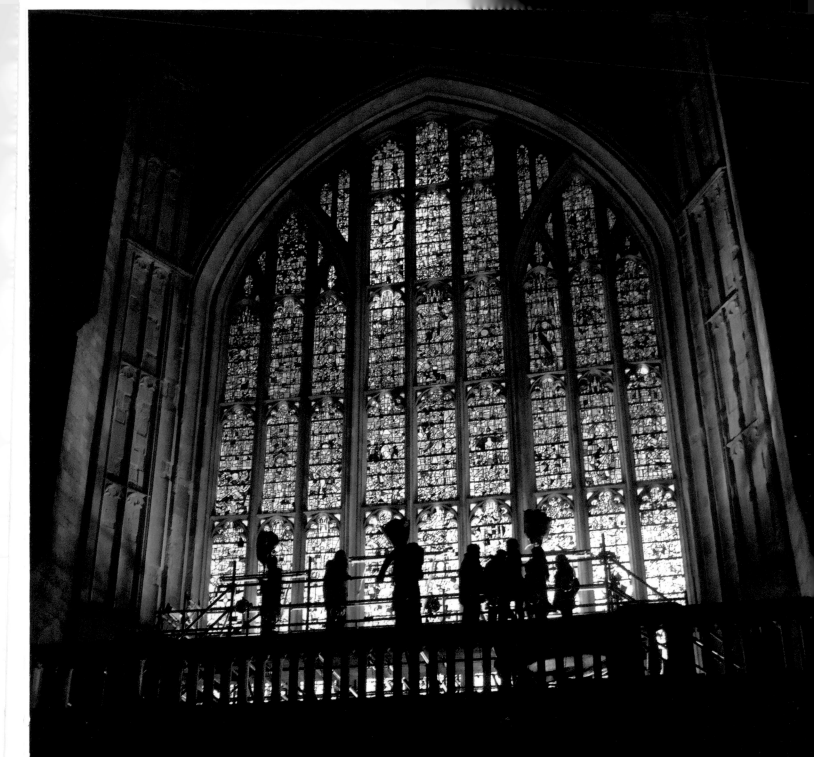

Testing the lights at the final rehearsal

It is often referred to as the Winchester Troper. A 'trope' means additions to the basic words of the service, usually sung, such as the introit, offertory, and communion. They fill out in a dramatic and musical way the Gospel story and the emotions the Gospel characters felt in the presence, in this case, of the resurrection. A troper is a book that contains such material. There are two copies of the Winchester Troper, one in Corpus Christi College Cambridge, and one in the British Library. The Librarian of Corpus Christi brought the Cambridge manuscript a few months ago to Winchester Cathedral, and the choir sang parts of the mass from it. The custom of setting words for saints days and for the great seasons of the church's year was widespread, but of all the written evidence about these tropers that give both words and actions of the Easter 'play', the Concordia version of Winchester is the oldest.

What follows is a description of the 'play' from the *Regularis Concordia*:

While the third lesson is being read, four of the brethren shall vest, one of whom wearing an alb as though for some different purpose, shall enter and go stealthily to the place of the 'sepulchre' and sit there quietly, holding a palm in his hand. Then, while the third respond is being sung, the other three brethren, vested in copes and holding thuribles in their hands, shall enter in the their turn and go to the place of the 'sepulchre', step by step, as though searching for something. Now these things are done in imitation of the angel seated on the tomb and of the women coming with perfumes to anoint the body of Jesus. When therefore, he that is seated shall see these three draw nigh, wandering about as it were and seeking something, he shall begin to sing softly and sweetly, *Quem quaeritis* (Whom do you seek?) As soon as this has been sung right through, the three shall answer together, *Ihesum Nazarenum* (Jesus of Nazareth). Then he that is seated shall say *Non est hic. Surrexit sicut praedixerat. Ite, nuntiate quia surrexit a mortuis* (He is not here. He has risen as he said. Go, announce that he is raised from the dead). At this command the three shall turn to the choir and saying *Alleluia. Resurrexit Dominus* (Alleluia. The Lord has risen). When this has been sung he that is seated, as though calling them back, shall say the Antiphon *Venite et videte locum*, (Come and see the place) and then, rising and lifting up the veil, he shall show them the place void of the Cross and with only the linen in which the Cross had been wrapped. Seeing this the three shall lay down their thuribles in that same 'sepulchre' and, taking the linen, shall hold it up before the clergy; and, as though showing that the Lord was risen and was no longer wrapped in it, they shall sing this antiphon: *Surrexit Dominus de sepulchro* (The Lord is risen from the tomb). They shall then lay the linen on the altar.

A CONJECTURAL view of SAXON WINCHESTER, CIRCA. A.D. 1000. LOOKING EAST

The trials begin

Caiaphas accuses Jesus

One of the camera teams from the University of Winchester

Herod: 'This is my throne.'

Looking at Jesus, Herodias asks Salome, 'Who do you say he is?'

Herod: 'If he is a king, then we must dress him like a king. In purple robes befitting his majesty!'

Pilate's wife arrives to warn him: 'Have nothing more to do with this good man.'

Pilate: 'Behold the man. Prisoner has undergone a Roman flogging. Surely now you are satisfied?'

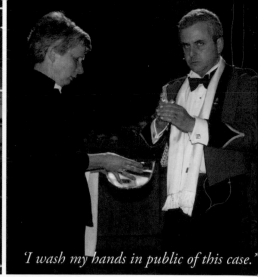

'I wash my hands in public of this case.'

Pilate: 'Release the murderer. Crucify the king.'

Barabbas: 'You've got the wrong man. It should have been me...'

7   The Cross Crucified
An Introduction to *The Dream of the Rood*

Kevin Crossley-Holland

KEVIN CROSSLEY-HOLLAND

Kevin Crossley-Holland is the prize winning author of the Arthur *trilogy. He is a poet and writer working prolifically in the area of myth and legend, drawing on the early Anglo-Saxon texts. He has translated* The Dream of the Rood, *a seventh-century poem about the crucifixion as experienced by the cross itself. He is an Honorary Fellow of St Edmund Hall, Oxford, a patron of the Sociey of Storytelling and a Fellow of the Royal Society of Literature.*

The poem that we are going to look at together begins with the injunction 'Hwæt!' 'Listen!'.

Hwæt, ic swefna cyst secgan wylle,
hwæt me gemaette to midre nihte …

I translated those lines when I was 23, and there wasn't much left to learn!

Listen! I will describe the best of dreams
which I dreamed in the middle of the night
when, far and wide, all men slept.

But before we come to *The Dream of the Rood*, let me remind you that many of the delightful Anglo-Saxon metaphorical riddles start *'ic wiht geseah'*. This means 'I saw a creature …' The riddler then goes on to describe something in terms that seem at first strange – but then you see through them, see *into* them. 'Quite true,' as Aristotle observed, in describing how a riddle works, 'quite true, and I'd missed the point.'

Just as, not very long ago, I borrowed – well, nicked actually – an apple from a headmistress' study and put it down on a table in front of a bunch of girls. 'Tell me something new about this apple,' I invited them.

'It will cry if you bite it,' one girl said.

'It's speckled,' said another.

And another: *'It's freckled.'*

'It's like a sphere,' said a fourth.

'What is a sphere?' I asked.

So she explained. And then a fifth girl volunteered, *'Well, it's got these pips inside it.'*

Mary Tudor, 1554

I want now to link Queen Elizabeth's visit to what comes next. Let's look at the symbolism of that Round Table in the Great Hall. Now this table was probably constructed at the end of the 13th century in either Henry III's reign or at the beginning of Edward II's. It was placed here in Winchester, which was reputed the actual site of Camelot, to underline the city's links with those ancient Arthurian ideals of chivalry. In Edward III's time, in 1344, the king had founded an Order of the Round Table, thinking this would be a valiant enterprise to bring his barons together and reestablish an age of glory and chivalry.

At the centre of this Round Table is a Tudor Rose. It was painted there in 1516 to mark the Tudor dynasty, derived by Henry VIII from his father, Henry VII. The rose has large red petals on the outside and small white ones on the inside. It was important that the red rose of Lancaster should dominate the white rose of York. Henry VII intended his claim to the throne to be established through his own birth line, and not owe anything to that of his queen, Elizabeth of York.

their captain similarly geared, was on horseback and when their pageant was about to be staged, the doors of the West End were flung open and there was a great volley of muskets, and smoke filled the cathedral. And then in rode this Captain on his horse and if you look at the picture you can just about see the horse. The soldiers carried pikes and they looked very threatening. The pikes were 17 foot high. I always think of this particularly because of the desecration done to the iconography, the shrines, the books, the vestments and the ornamentation within cathedrals and churches. A 17 foot pike can reach very far.

After that, we had the boys again from Winchester College going through an eighteenth century bishop's life. Benjamin Hoadly was Bishop of Winchester from 1734–61 and he was a controversial theologian living in Chelsea but there is no evidence that he ever actually visited Winchester. So the boys went to town on this with great style. The last scene was by the Nave altar. A screen had been raised and the people who had taken part were facing West and the audience was facing east, and on the screen was shown how the Queen had been occupied in Winchester on that day, on Maundy Thursday in 1979. She had been photographed in detail as she progressed through from the morning service to the grand luncheon and to the formal farewell. So that was our celebration in 1979.

The Round Table at Winchester Great Hall

*Players and audience at the marriage of
Mary Tudor and Philip of Spain*

Overview of the roof bosses at Norwich Cathedral

images of Herod, might also reflect the thought that Richard III himself killed those children.

While on the other hand Henry VII wished himself to be seen as the new Moses who had led his people through the troubled times of the York-Lancastrian wars towards the peace and prosperity of an era over which a new King Arthur would reign.

Much of that type/antitype pattern informs the late fifteenth and early sixteenth century roof bosses of Norwich Cathedral. And the stories of these roof bosses relate closely to the drama of that period.

There are 1,100 stone carved roof bosses in Norwich Cathedral, and the majority of them are story-telling. And they tell the Christian story: of the Old Testament and the New, of the saints, and beyond that, of much folk and apocryphal material as well.

There was a fire in the roof in the middle of the 15th century, and a stone ribbed vaulting was constructed, and in the nave we have about 250 roof bosses. The first seven bays, from the east, deal with Old Testament subjects and the next seven bays deal with the New Testament and there is a relation between them. It's not meticulous, it's not consistent, but there is that type/anti-type pattern which I mentioned earlier, such as the crossing of the Red Sea, and the Harrowing of Hell.

One of the first bosses depicts the Creation. This is late 15th century, God the Father creates the universe and in his hand he holds his dividers. This is a form of the Trinity, with the unicorn and the lion. And the creation of Adam, and the creation of Eve as Adam sleeps. At this time, also in Norwich, you have a St Luke's Guild which was responsible for the plays in Norwich. By 1527 and the years that follow, the Grocers were responsible for the play of Adam and Eve. Now that is the only extant play we have, in fact we have two redacted versions of it, but we also have the Grocers' accounts for these 16th century years. The accounts are fascinating, one item is 'a rib coloured red' and so we know what that is for – it is a theatrical 'prop' for the creation of Eve.

And for the Temptation, the Fall in the garden, we can relate how these roof boss images have something to do with the drama of the time. There are lots of apples on this tree but it is, as it were, a continuous handing-out of apples. Satan hands one to Eve and she hands one to Adam but if you look at Satan, Satan has a feminine appearance. And I know that the figure of the tempter or The Stranger in your Winchester Passion picks up on this tradition. It was quite common in the Middle Ages to think that all evil came from the female sex.

And here is the Harrowing of Hell with the jaws of Hell and at this moment when Christ comes to Hell, Christ challenges Satan and then draws out of Hell Adam and Eve, and the prophets, who have been waiting in limbo all these years for this moment of redemption. Where this gets very interesting for me is where you have a play, as in the N-Town Play, which shows the sealing of the tomb (unique in medieval drama) and you get a carving which is very, very scarce but present in the Norwich cloisters. And what happens in the sealing of the tomb is that Pilate and his knights and his soldiers on one side of the tomb and Annas and Caiaphas and the priests on the other, and they are coming to seal the tomb in which Christ has been buried. It is not a cave tomb you can see, it is a 14th/ 15th century tomb, and they want to put seals on it to stop Christ rising. And here is the bag of wax and here is Pilate probably about to seal the tomb as are Annas and Caiaphas, and here you can see the clasp on the tomb.

And here is Mary Magdalene coming to the tomb to anoint the dead Christ. From her wrist hangs an alabaster casket. When she meets the resurrected Christ she doesn't recognize him. When he speaks her name she falls to his feet, his wounded feet, to anoint them and to dry them with her hair. You need to view this boss from different angles to appreciate the full story that it intends to convey. The artist interprets this moment with an imaginative intensity beyond biblical authority. The art of the Middle Ages is characterized by such flashes of creative genius, at the hand of the carver or in the plays of the butcher, the baker, the candle-stick maker.

On 13 March 1965 I drove from Yorkshire to Winchester for an interview. When I left the West Riding the weather was fine. When I reached Hampshire it was snowing heavily. On the evening of Good Friday, 21 March, 2008, under that full moon, the Winchester Passion will be presented. The weather will play a part, as it should. But the event will eclipse the weather when, in your streets, you tell that old story once again in a way it has never quite been told before.

Three prisoners take up their cross-beams and begin the march to Golgotha.

Prisoners are paraded for public ridicule at the Buttercross

After Jesus falls, Simon of Cyrene is pulled from the crowd to help him carry the cross

A Stranger in red taunts Jesus

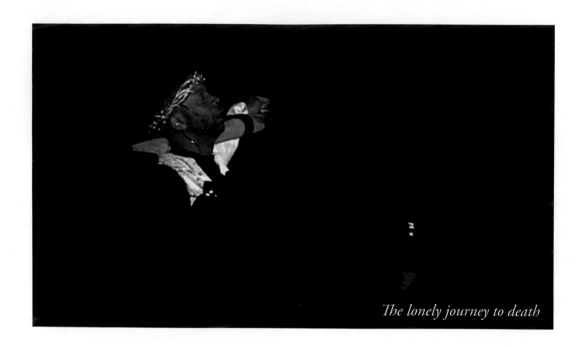

The lonely journey to death

9   Televising the Passion

Adam Kemp

ADAM KEMP

Adam Kemp is the BBC's Commissioner for Arts, Music, Performance and Religion. He is responsible for programmming these genres across all four BBC television networks. He has executive-produced more than eighty factual series and specials, including the Emmy and Bafta award-winning Walking With Dinosaurs *specials. His recent commissions include* The Manchester Passion, Liverpool Nativity, Seven Ages Of Rock, Genius Of Photography, The Story Of God, Extreme Pilgrim *and* How We Built Britain.

When I started this job, I think the time was ripe for a resurgence and renaissance in religious television. In fact, within a few days of my starting (I was commissioning across both in-house productions and the independent sector) Pope John Paul II died, and you will remember those weeks were quite astonishing. It felt as if the entire world was debating religion, leadership and issues of moral authority. And of course behind that lay the big issues of coming to terms with Islamism post 9/11 and the desperate hunger for information about all religions. Plus some really alarming statistics about ignorance in our quite secular society about what Easter, for example, was about.

There was a sense in which our Judeo-Christian culture was not so accessible to many of our young people. Yet equally at the same time, there were all the signs, particularly amongst the young, of a quest and a hunger for insight into spirituality, their inner life, ethics, and morality.

So we did (as it were) a school report, on how the BBC, a leader in religious broadcasting, was doing. The verdict had that slightly familiar ring of 'could do better' and of course we are still guided by these wonderful three Reithian principles – to inform, to educate and to entertain.

As we moved towards more innovation, we remained totally committed to classic forms of story-telling. We have myriad audiences to serve: we have believers of many kinds, non-believers of many kinds too, viewers and listeners of all generations. And we wanted to use this toolkit of television, its formats, its genres, to reach out for more.

And this is where *The Manchester Passion* came in. It was on BBC 3, which

The Manchester Passion cast, 2006
Left to right: Keith Allen: Narrator and Pontias Pilate, Darren Morfitt: Jesus, Tim Booth: Judas, Nicholas Bailey: Peter

is a key plank of the BBC's youth mission. And the team that created it were actually from the Classical Music Department. You may recall a programme called *Flashmob Opera* that preceded it and was award-winning too. It was there that they learnt new skills and became interested in a 'live' and quite dangerous style of broadcasting.

The genesis was quite extraordinary. Of course the team were absolutely aware of the Mystery Plays. They were fully conscious of those influences and the great traditions of Bach and religious music making. Very quickly, though, they joined forces with the religious department to begin thinking about how we could do something more, given that we wanted to tackle the Passion story.

The programme that you saw was not the programme we originally set out to do. There was a completely extraordinary and I think an inspired moment – an 'eureka' moment – from one of the producers soon after we had made the decision to move it to Manchester. He was also a keen student of modern popular music; this is the point. He was part of our Classical Music Department but he knew, like many of us, the great strengths of that city's popular music: Oasis and the like. And from studying and knowing the lyrics of these modern popular songs, he said, 'I think that we can actually tell the Passion story through this music'.

And I remember thinking, well, that is completely astonishing – we looked over the lyrics in the cold light of day. Truly, it is something I would recommend to you. There was enormous beauty and power in those songs. Pick a band like The Stone Roses and you will see that spirituality is deeply embedded in their lyrics.

So now we had, if you like, 'the big idea'. In television we are always hungry not just to inform, educate and entertain but to do the 'next big thing'. To innovate, to take risks and thereby get noticed. But I remember we were talking earlier this morning about your worries about the weather for your event in Winchester? That definitely is a worry for outside broadcasts. But this was terrifying; I have to tell you, because the scale of this outside broadcast was incredible. There were teams in different areas of the city and the sound was being bounced off walls to satellite dishes, and the concern about whether it would stay synchronised frankly kept me awake for much of the night. We were confident of its originality, and we had fabulous support from the local churches who were deeply involved – their congregations were carrying the Cross.

Yet, we were quite uncertain how well the event would be received. There was a sense in which this could be seen as quite dangerous. As it turned out, I have to say, it was a deeply moving experience. I even feel moved watching the clip again. The city centre was completely closed down. There were the church congregations, every generation indeed, and a huge number of young Mancunians who were both excited and taking enormous pride in their own city's creative achievements in music and culture.

And so *The Manchester Passion* is really a hard one to top. It did get on air on television, it might have been a disaster but it worked.

It did something very interesting for us, and not just for our young audience. We also found the press were writing leader articles about a new form of worship which, I swear, we had not anticipated. That was wonderfully exciting.

The Liverpool Nativity, which we did recently, was always set up as the 'twin'. We'd done The Passion and The Nativity was an obvious story to follow. Again, look at the strength of Liverpool's music and culture – and of course, 2008 was Liverpool's year as Capital of European Culture.

We are fortunate to have four TV networks: *The Private Life of A Masterpiece* played on BBC2, *The Manchester Passion* was on BBC3 and was also shown again on BBC2, whilst *The Liverpool Nativity* was repeated on BBC1 (we wanted to share it with wider audiences and BBC1 and BBC2 reach millions).

The very specific brief I have is to develop new types of religious programming beyond *Songs of Praise* and our worship programmes right in the heart of BBC1? That is a big ask, and this is where drama comes in. The backbone of BBC1 is its drama output, so I think it was inevitable that we would come back to look at the Passion as a drama.

I don't know about you, but I still vividly remember Robert Powell's eyes when he played Jesus of Nazareth. What an astonishing impact that series had. I think the

My first feature film for the cinema, *Man Dancin'* was referred to by a critic as a cross between *On the Waterfront*, *The Godfather III* and *Jesus of Montreal*. And I thought, 'Okay, that's nice. I'll accept that'. It was an allegorical Passion story. The idea was to place the central figure in modern-day Glasgow. He's an ex-criminal coming out of jail having had his life changed, having actually found faith while in jail, but coming back to a world where everyone thinks he must be up to no good, and starting his own gang.

In the middle of all that, in order to avoid the rather touchy-feely anger-management groups, he has the option to act in a Passion play. So he gets involved in that and ends up having to run the whole thing, a very revolutionary event in the centre of Glasgow. At the same time, the greater story around it is also a Passion play. It is a complicated, violent little story which accentuates the bloodiness of it all, as did Mel Gibson, and which we have tended to gloss over.

I came out shell-shocked like everyone else when I went to a preview of Mel Gibson's *The Passion of the Christ*, but I found it very moving and I cried in it. I was brought up very much in the Protestant tradition and I think we

have neglected Mary in this, and there are some wonderful moments with that very good actress who played Mary. But it was also very shocking in its violence.

However, even though it was shocking, I was very grateful that it broke the 'stained glass window' to which we often confine Jesus... and we can all be guilty of that. We all want Him to be nice, but Jesus wasn't nice. He wasn't beige. think the power of that film – even though there were excesses – smashed through the stained glass window and put Jesus back in the high street.

I do youth work, and certainly some of the young people I work with were bowled over by it, and it gave them a different slant. It was a powerful piece of well-crafted film and it started a debate which I hope will go on forever.

The story is strong, elemental, and I am really interested in this Winchester Passion that you are about to do. Why do we go on telling this story? It is powerful, it resonates and if you can step out of the stained glass window into the high street – which you are obviously doing, by literally going out onto the streets of your city – I think the world can be your oyster.

I think the story of Jesus really does communicate to people, and if all these churches we see scattering the landscape are to be believed, then it is pretty much the most important story around. There is an amazing appetite for it and I think you will get a tremendous response for it. Mel Gibson didn't so do badly with his blood-fest version, did he? Huge numbers of people wanted to see it, and that's good. And you know people will want to see another one, and another one, because it speaks deeply to the human condition.

Each film maker wants to make his own film. Pasolini was a socialist and so his film presented a very political Jesus, a man of the people. Zeffirelli's vision was very different. That is what happens – you can only ever tell a corner of the story. Or you can come at it very obliquely, like with *Man Dancin'* where you are creating a sort of allegory and that can sometimes be more powerful than approaching it 'full on'. As my good friend Murray Watts says, 'What art can do is to make people feel so much, they can't help but think,' and that's it, that is my motto.

The first of the prisoners is crucified

A defiant shout from the 'terrorist': 'Death to the Romans!'

The Stranger taunts Jesus

'It is finished.'

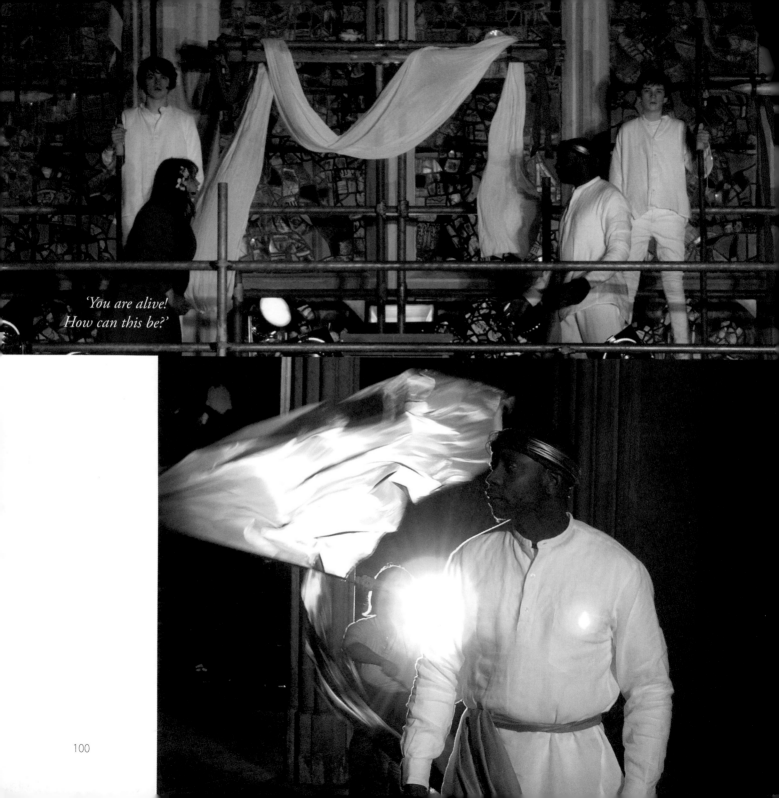

'You are alive!
How can this be?'

100

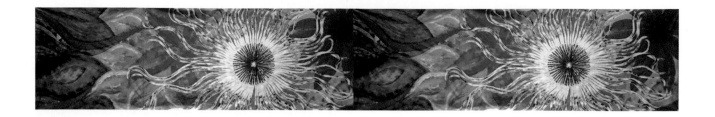

11

After the Passion

Mark Byford and others

MARK BYFORD is Deputy Director General of the BBC and head of all its journalism. As Chair of the BBC's Journalism Board, he has overall responsibility for the world's largest and most trusted news organisation providing extensive news and current affairs services across radio, television and interactive media for the UK and the world. His responsibilities also include BBC Sport and Editorial Policy. He is also Chair of the BBC's Editorial Standards Board responsible for promoting the highest standards in ethics and programme-making across the BBC; Chair of the BBC Complaints Management Board responsible for the efficient and effective handling of complaints across the Corporation; Chair of the Learning Board responsible for developing training and staff development across the BBC; and Chair of the BBC's London 2012 Olympic Games Coordinating Group.

There is no doubt about it: the Winchester Passion created a real buzz across the city and indeed around the county.

When the concept was first launched, in a packed Winchester Cathedral, you could feel the huge level of enthusiasm – indeed passion – that was already being generated for it. There was a real sense of both challenge and ambition; recognising an opportunity for reaching out to the community, combined with an appetite for teams from different walks of life to work together to make the idea a reality.

I live on Oram's Arbour, so the Passion's opening on Good Friday evening took place literally on my doorstep! We're used to seeing a crowded Arbour for the Hat Fair picnic each July. What was so gratifying was to see an equally huge crowd come together for such an important day in the Christian calendar, to witness the story of the Passion.

It's something I will never forget. And the journey to the Law Courts, and then down Winchester High Street to the Cathedral, worked so well in theatrical terms in bringing the story alive.

As the event's Patron, I feel proud and privileged to have played a small part in getting the Winchester Passion off the ground, supporting it from the launch to its very successful outcome.

I witnessed a lot of people working so hard and collaboratively over many months to make it happen. We owe them all a huge debt.

Most importantly, I was particularly delighted to see the event acting as a catalyst for different Christian denominations in the area to come together so publicly to support the venture … and I hope that will be its lasting legacy.

A MOTHER'S VIEW

I am the mother of 'James the elder' and his brother. No, not John this time (as in the Bible) but Tim the technician. For me, the Winchester Passion was a moving experience as both my sons were involved, and living the experience of the Passion story as they had never done before.

My eldest son, playing the role of a disciple, said that he had tasted the bonds which held those first disciples together, and the awe that they had for their leader, Jesus. My younger son felt honoured to become the personal technical assistant to Israel, following him closely throughout the performance, carrying his water and holding his microphone during costume changes. The experience of pushing through the crowds to keep up with Jesus is one he will not forget.

I had never really noticed the mother mentioned briefly in Matthew's Gospel before. But as I stood in the crowd, I became her. 'Then the mother of Zebedee's sons came to Jesus with her sons and, kneeling down, asked a favour of him. "What is it you want?" he asked. She said, "Grant that one of these two sons of mine may sit at your right and the other at your left in your kingdom."' (Matthew 20, 20-21.) How often have I prayed for the best for my sons, not really knowing what it is? Yes, I could identify with that mother, that night, as I stood there trying to understand the Passion.

Christine Slatcher

A MILESTONE EXPERIENCE

I am writing to say how extraordinarily powerful it was, and an amazing witness on Good Friday, as over 10,000 people flooded into Winchester. There was a tremendous atmosphere generated by the combination of the Passion Play and the huge crowds. It really did create a sense of Jerusalem at Passover.

It was a venture of faith, a huge undertaking, a milestone experience and a very special Good Friday witness.

Very Revd James Attwell
Dean of Winchester Cathedral

FROM THE BLIND SIDE

With words and actions about to reach their climax,
And all fallen strangely quiet,
We stood anonymously alongside neighbours.

Then from the blind side it came, addressing pretences,
Attacking prejudices and demanding attention.

Cutting harder than any two-edged sword, it
Sliced through the cold night air, puncturing
The distance from scaffold to crowd.

Was it my imagination or were there some present
Who reeled back under its force?

Inviting language should have been warning of
What was to come . . . 'Roll-up! Roll-Up!'
But there was no time to retreat.

'Roll-up . . . for the *entertainment!*'
Clinically sharp and cold as steel, the word
Jostled and jarred expectations.

It unmasked hearts and levered minds:
Is it nothing more than this, all you that pass by?

One of the Crowd

THOUSANDS WATCH PASSION PLAY

WINCHESTER PASSION

Street theatre is set to be 'once in a lifetime' spectacle

PRESS AND MEDIA REVIEWS

Thousands of people packed the streets of Winchester on Good Friday as the cathedral city's most famous locations played host to a spectacular recreation of the Easter story.

Winchester was taken back to the days of Roman-occupied Jerusalem as the Winchester Passion told the Easter story around the city's historic locations – Oram's Arbour, the Great Hall, Law Courts, Westgate, Buttercross and of course, the cathedral.

A captivating performance by Israel Oyelumade as Jesus led a cast of the key characters in the story of the days leading up to Jesus' crucifixion.

The 12 disciples, Pontius Pilate, Herod and the temple priests had a supporting cast of professional and amateur actors, musicians and dancers drawn from all walks of life in the city.

Inspired by the Manchester Passion of 2006, the Winchester Passion was written by Philip Glassborow and was an ambitious project to bring together Winchester churches along with community groups, Winchester University, Winchester Community Choir, youth and student groups.

Although the idea of Passion plays goes back to medieval 'Mystery Plays', the Winchester Passion was given modern media twists – BBC Radio Solent presenter Tim Daykin played the part of the narrator, a TV news anchorman bringing breaking news of the story to the audience.

Staging a play at outdoor locations around the city was no mean logistical feat and was achieved with the support of the Army, BBC South, the city council and a team of technicians who used more than 50 radio microphones to cover the action as it moved through the city.

Three giant outdoor screens relayed the scenes to the massed crowds – thought to number over 10,000 – as the story unfolded.

The play started at Oram's Arbour with Jesus' entrance into the city on a donkey. The rain clouds gathered – but the predicted rain did not come – and the audiences swelled at all the outdoor locations despite the biting March cold.

The tide of people flowed down towards Winchester's Great Hall where the party at Lazarus' house and the Last Supper were played out along with Judas Iscariot's fateful decision to betray Jesus.

The law courts and sculpture garden were the apt locations for Jesus' trial by the Temple Pharisees, Pontius Pilate eventually washing his hands of Jesus and the crowd calling for the freeing of Barabas.

Winchester's High Street became the Via Dolorosa as Jesus began his journey carrying his cross down the hill towards the Buttercross.

The floodlit cathedral was the spectacular setting for the Passion's emotionally-charged ending when Jesus was put to death on the balcony high above the audience on the Cathedral Green who looked on transfixed.

The crucifixion and resurrection scenes were accompanied by a new composition of Adoremus – A Winchester Prayer by Sir John Tavener performed in the cathedral by the Waynflete Singers and Southern Voices.

Writer Philip Glassborow was pleased with the event: 'It's been a roller coaster of joys and delights. Wonderful things have happened and on the whole it has been incredible.'

'There were long dialogue scenes but people were listening and it really seems that people were taking it on board.'

The Bishop of Winchester, Michael Scott-Joynt, said: 'I found it a remarkable evening. The group of people, originally quite a small group of Winchester ministers have been brave enough to embark on this astonishing project.

'My prayers will be about what God may be working in all these folk as they reflect on what they've seen.'

Indy Almroth-Wright and Stephen Stafford,
BBC Hampshire website

More than 10,000 people braved near-freezing conditions as one of the most eye-catching pieces of street theatre attempted in Britain came to Winchester.

With a cast of nearly 300, and a similar number of technicians and stewards, along with music, large screens and special effects, this was a night for the city to remember...

The play was performed using modern costume and dialogue, in the hope of making it accessible to all. The show, which lasted nearly three hours, was also free, with churches across Winchester working together to raise more than £50,000 to stage the piece . . .

With hundreds of cast and crew, the Army volunteered to set up a field kitchen to keep everyone working on the show fed and watered.

Bus operator, Stagecoach, ran extra evening services to cope with the demand generated by the play.

Warwick Payne, Hampshire Chronicle

LOST CHILDREN

'It's cold and late, darling. I'll read you the story tomorrow.'
'Daddy, I know the story.'

This exchange, overheard in Winchester Cathedral Close some time after eight o'clock on a freezing Good Friday night, summed up the nature of the Winchester Passion, performed this year for the first, but surely not the last, time.

It was a huge civic event and communal experience. Naturally it combined many elements. It retold the events of Good Friday more or less as recounted in the Gospels. It wore its evangelical heart on its sleeve. It exploited the large (although on this occasion, not always large enough) public spaces with which Winchester is especially blessed. It brought together, on a scale that created some problems, young and old, believer and non-believer, the fit, the halt and the lame, to say nothing of the dogs. But people were generally good-humoured and as the event ended, the 'Lost Children' tent was happily redundant . . .

Many watchers were clearly unacquainted with the reality of live theatre, let alone live theatre performed in packed streets, squares and fields. Some were outraged that, packed together with taller, fatter or less considerate people, they had a less than perfect view . . .

Yet for considerable periods, the audience was concentratedly silent. The temptation of Judas was one such moment, as were scenes involving Pilate and all those with the show's one professional actor, Israel Oyelumade. He had a physical and vocal presence that compelled attention...

The evening began with a local festival – brass band, diminutive gymnast, morris dancers – on Oram's Arbour, a hillside park west of the city, the centre of Winchester when the Romans arrived. Blue skies had several times given way to lashing winds and rain. This happened one last time precisely as the play began: Passover preparations had to be glimpsed through a canopy of umbrellas.

The courtyards of the Great Hall and Law Courts accommodated events from the raising of Lazarus to the trial; the High Street became the Via Dolorosa; and the balcony on the west front of the Cathedral was Golgotha. There were interludes of dance and song, including a new work by Sir John Tavener: *Adoremus, The Winchester Prayer*... Few who were present will forget the event, even those who choose not to embrace its slogan and 'Walk the Way'.

Tom Aitken

THOUSANDS WATCH PASSION PLAY

Herod was played as a blustering braggart, unsettled by the mysterious silence of Jesus. Pontius Pilate, dressed as an army officer in evening mess kit, was portrayed as a sympathetic character, unable in the end to reconcile the unfathomable

Jesus with the righteous anger of the Jewish religious elite. When the crowd and the audience called for Barabbas rather than Jesus to be freed, he washed his hands of the whole affair.

The High Street then became the Via Dolorosa, as Jesus was hustled to his crucifixion. This last act had a magnificent setting, high up on the west front of the Cathedral. One of the thieves said, 'Jesus, remember me, when you come into your kingdom,' and gently the crowd took up the chant.

Israel Oyelumade, the actor who played Jesus, was left alone and in agony. A red-jacketed woman tempter urged him to save himself . . . With awe-inspring majesty, Jesus overcame even his sense of complete abandonment by God.

As he died, enormous speakers recreated the earthquake and the tearing of the temple veil.

Throughout this scene, in the cold sky above the Cathedral a bright full moon had shone. At the moment of Jesus's death, a dagger of dark cloud drifted across it.

Angels danced on the big screen, before the risen Jesus appeared to Mary Magdalene... As the magnificent truth dawned, Mary, like the audience, was left amazed and overawed.

Portsmouth People

SOME COMMENTS FROM CAST AND CREW

I was blessed to play Veronica, such an intimate and beautiful role which had huge personal meaning to me. The night of the play was very precious. Walking amongst the crowds, carrying within my heart the secret of knowing what I was about to do at the Buttercross.

When I saw Israel coming towards me out of the crowd, everything and everyone else vanished. No-one had warned me about the blood! I was truly stunned by the state of him. And then, in a moment, I knew that I was seeing Jesus. Israel was still Israel, but Jesus was there too. Not a triumphant, powerful Jesus, but a real man, bleeding and beaten in every way. I was completely overwhelmed . . .

The thud of wood bruised her heart,
the helpless falling
drew her pain
like splinters from a wound.
Healed herself, she longed
to heal his bloodied form.

Once, she had touched
the hem of his robe.
Now, she dared
to touch his face.
Compassion made her reach
to draw
the splinters of his pain.

Lynda Price

The whole experience has been very special: the formation of friendships, the dedication of the directors, the admirable administration by Dorothy, the terrific teas and homely hospitality of the Vineyard Church tea-lady. And behind the stage curtain, each person playing their own special part as unsung heroes . . .

Michael Beurlen

I was in charge of the 'execution detail' escorting Jesus, Dymas and Gestas from the Law Courts down to the Buttercross and on to the Cathedral.

It was freezing cold but the earlier hail and rain had gone, and the High Street was lined with people all the way to the Buttercross. Some were shouting, some said nothing as we went by. However, the full moon was up and out, in line perfectly with the procession.

Despite the hubbub and colour and noise on the surface, there was a dark silence in the stark, white light of the moon. There was the past, the present and future, all there at once. What we were doing that evening had been done for hundreds of years and would be done for hundreds more to come, within communities all over the world, with their full moon in their night sky . . .

Rupert Cazalet

A special memory felt by the 'disciples' was the relationship that we quickly developed with the audience, and the impromptu conversations that we and Jesus held with the audience when we were waiting for Act Two to begin. This also gave Jesus the opportunity to talk to the people around him, and introducing him to a group of children was very special. There was a real festival feeling everywhere. It was also fascinating to see the reaction of happy, smiling people with hands outstretched, that visibly retracted on hearing me say, 'Greetings, my name is Judas'.

Stephen Gleed

I've just got back from the West Front of the Cathedral and simply must write to you and say what a truly splendid and passionate event this has been... Abigail and I were in the front row for the trial scenes and the atmosphere was utterly amazing, and so powerful... I've just put Abigail to bed (having first defrosted her with a cup of cocoa) and we started a 'thank you' prayer for those taking part, and we just kept on thinking of more and more people who must have made all this possible – writers, singers, dancers, actors, musicians, stewards, costume designers/makers, props, painters, army, cameramen, sound, light, technicians, designers, drivers, gofers, police, publicity, coordinators, pray-ers, builders, H&S, liaisons, administrators, the list just goes on!

Brilliant, brilliant, brilliant. Thank you all so much for the year of effort and stress you have put in.

Sophie Hacker

COMMENTS FROM THE BBC WEBSITE

The atmosphere was electric as people watched, captivated by the well played scenes. I enjoyed the 'modern meets ancient' dynamic of the play and thought that Israel did an amazing job. Well done to everyone.

With part of the action taking place through the crowd, you actually felt part of the crowd in Jerusalem; we nearly got knocked over by Roman soldiers dragging one of the terrorists off to jail. Altogether a fantastic achievement which made one realise that these things really happened – and made one ask 'Why?'

I went because I was curious to see how such a huge undertaking of street theatre would be managed. I found myself staying for the rest of the night, finding it a thought-provoking, challenging and ultimtely praiseworthy event. The crowds around me were respectful and interested. There were no barriers in the street, people just made way for the actors when they passed. Despite thousands of people, I wasn't jostled, asked for money, or pressured into any beliefs. I went home feeling happy that I'd seen an unusual event in my city. I congratulate everyone involved: the actors – who had rehearsed their roles – and most of all the people around me that night – who hadn't rehearsed.

It was an amazing performance, using our city as the stage. This is what Easter is about for the Christian community, but never for a moment did I feel that it excluded me. There was a drama unfolding in our streets and it had a raw quality that was enthralling.

Congratulations to all the stewards who did a fantastic job. We were advised to go straight to the law courts and had a good

Sarah Morgan conducting

Part of The Passion Chorale

view of one of the large screens, could hear well and could see parts of the trial scenes. Our 7 year old daughter stuck it out to the end and has been asking lots of questions. A unique and exciting experience for all of us. Thanks...

My son and I decided to follow the entire production from Oram's Arbour right down to the cathedral. At times it was difficult to see the actors and even the screen but we kept moving forward everywhere we went and saw more of the production than not. We ran down the high street after the actors thereby getting a fantastic view as we found ourselves walking right next to Israel all the way to the cathedral for a front row view...

Ewen Huffman, Technology Producer

A brilliant event. It was very pleasing to witness so many people attending the event and giving it due concentration and reverence. It was a biting cold evening and both the actors in their scanty costumes, as well as the audience, were coping with the cold, though I am sure Salome must have been frozen. Just one plea – bigger screens next time, please!

I thought I would listen to just the first part on the radio to see what it would be like and ended up being absolutely captivated by the production.

Although we couldn't see much it was a very good experience being there, and we were very impressed by the organisation of such a complex and large event. We finished by going home and following the rest of it on Radio Solent in the warmth of our home. The story came across well on radio with effective presentation. It was a moving evening.

Thank you and congratulations in taking the Leap of Faith to put on the Passion. Ten thousand people, what a crowd! We were towards the back so didn't see very much but the large screens were great and the atmosphere truly inspiring. I had seen the three crosses being erected at the Cathedral a week or so before and they sent shivers down my spine! Congratulations again. Next time I want to take part – hooray and well done, or should I say Halelluia!!

We were frozen, but very moved, not only by the events, the acting, and the dedication of the actors, but mainly to be amongst so many Christians or people seeking to know more. Some scenes were difficult to get near but we were able to get a place at the Cathedral and the sight of the last scenes in front of the stained glass window of the Cathedral will stay with me always. Thank you everyone for staging this in this wonderful setting.

I found it an awesome experience seeming so real. There were moments of emotion, anger, sadness and glimpses of humour which made it all the more spectacular. To see the huge turn out of every age gave me great new hope for the Christian faith, and most noticeable was the good behaviour; people listened intently with an atmosphere of great expectation. A superb experience. I was glad to be there. Thank you to all who made it possible.

Photograph by Katie Williams

Judy's passion for play is a winner

Artist Judy Strafford and Winchester Passion co-ordinator, The Rev Doctor Howard Mellor, with the publicity material she produced for the performance. T8522B

AN Easton painter said she was "thrilled" after having her artwork chosen for next month's Winchester Passion festival.

Judy Strafford's painting of Jesus among the city's landmarks will feature on publicity for the event, which will be sent to around 25,000 homes in the district.

The open-air play is a modern dramatisation of the betrayal and crucifixion of Jesus followed by the resurrection and ascension.

Her piece, a large oil painting on canvas, has the son of God against a backdrop of landmarks such as Winchester Cathedral, the Buttercross and the Guildhall.

Lady Strafford said the project took her six weeks to complete.

The lifelong artist said: "I was particularly pleased because I felt I was happy with it. But then there's that horrendous moment when the people who commissioned it had to see it. But they loved it.

"I'm immensely proud of it. I'm thrilled to pieces about the whole thing — it's going to be a fantastic event, there's so much effort gone into it."

Lady Strafford said the hardest part came after the painting was finished, when organisers told her Jesus had to be black, rather than white.

She added "I knew I could do it (alter the painting) but it was very testing, probably the most testing part of it all!"

More information about the Winchester Passion, which is on Friday, March 21, is available on www.thewinchesterpassion.org.uk.

Hampshire Chronicle

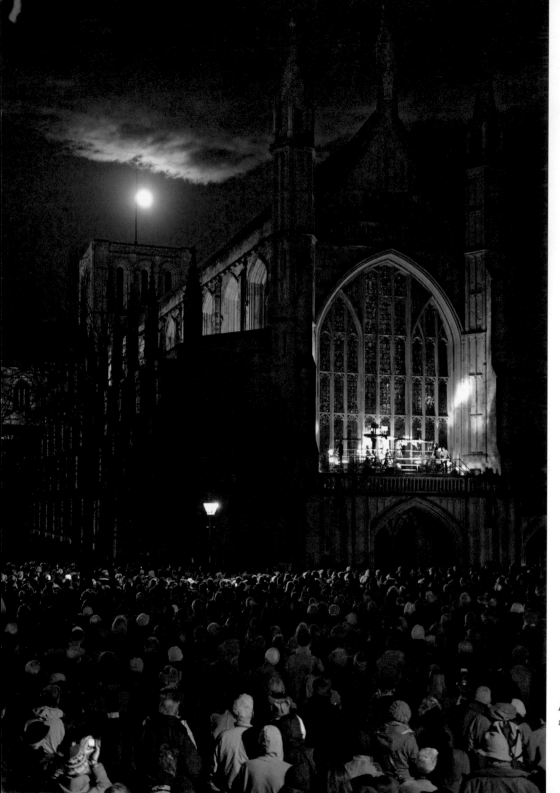

Photograph by Joe Low
www.joelow.com

THE WINCHESTER PASSION

The Producers and Directors would like to give thanks for the expertise, dedication, hard work and good humour of the hundreds of people who have worked on the many teams to make this event possible. Above all we thank God for His goodness and grace throughout and our prayer is that this production brings glory to the Lord Jesus Christ and draws people closer to Him.

Patron   Mark Byford,
Deputy Director-General of the BBC

Supporters   Colin Firth
Howard Goodall

Producers
Revd Dr Howard Mellor, The United Church (Chair)
Revd David Williams, Christ Church
Revd Ewen Huffman, Winchester Baptist Church
Revd Dr Roland Riem, Winchester Cathedral
Yvonne Secker
Jeremy Davis

Written by Matthew, Mark, Luke, John,
and Philip Glassborow

Incorporating the World Premiere of a new commission:
ADOREMUS – The Winchester Prayer by Sir John Tavener.
Performed by the Waynflete Singers and Southern Voices,
conducted by Andrew Lumsden. Organist, Philip White-Jones.
Producer, Sarah Baldock.

Drama Directors
Neil Simpson (Act 1)
Geoffrey Burnaby (Act 2)
David Simpkin (Act 3)
Philip Glassborow (Act 4)
Cecily O'Neill (Act 5)

Project Management
Juli Wills and Naomi Honey

Directors
Camera Director – Paul Carter
Company Director – Peter Smith
Costume & Wardrobe – Marjory Monro, Llyn Parker and
Melanie Tibbitts

Decor and banners – Helene Bevan
Fundraising – Peter Russell
Health & Safety Director – Roland Burberry
Music Director – Carl Clausen
Outreach Director – Peter Davey
Power & Lighting Director – Doug Bennett
Prayer Directors – Helen Revans, Geoff & Angela Vaine
Production Director – Michael Orpen-Palmer
Publicity Director – Mike Simpson
Schools Team Director – Laura Chase
Site Director – Fred Randall
Sound Director – Steve Lucas
Staging Director – Lorna Browne
Stewards & Security Director – Ray Cousins
Technology Director – Ken Liddell
Website – Matt Howson

Associate Directors
Professor June Boyce-Tillman (Step Into The Picture project)
Jo Burnaby (props)
Phil Clee (Via Dolorosa)
Anna Gillibrand (company manager)
Elizabeth Glassborow (Gethsemane Blues)
Debbie Lee-Anthony (choreography)
Dorothy Lusmore (production administrator)
Annie McKean (University of Winchester liaison)
Dirk Maggs (sound effect design)
Sarah Morgan (Winchester Community Choir/The Passion Chorale)
Tim Robbins (auditions)
David & Miggy Scott ('Presenting the Passion' symposium)
Philip Tutt-Leppard (media)
Hannah Williams (University Gospel Choir)

Artistic Credits
Blue Apple Theatre Company
Christ Church Worship Group (Leader Chris Kipling)
D@Win Dance
Hamble Area Youth Band (Conducted by Julie Farnel and Mark Streather)
Salvation Army Band
Southern Voices
The University Gospel Choir
The Waynflete Singers
Winchester Community Choir
Winchester Morris Men
Winchester Young Voices (Conductor Nick Sims)

CAST AND CREW

Jesus of Nazareth a teacher	*Israel Oyelumade*	**Herod's Bodyguards**	*Tristan Mason-Smith*
			Ian Dighe
Simon Peter a fisherman	*Michael Alborough*	**Annas** high priest	*Arthur Croad*
		Caiaphas chief priest	*David Lea*
Andrew his brother	*Paul Robinson*	**Nicodemus** a Pharisee of the Sanhedrin	*Andy Hider*
John 'Boanerges'	*Ryan Connolly-Moore*	**Joseph of Arimathea**	*Philip Tutt-Leppard*
James 'Boanerges'	*Sam Slatcher*	**Jairus** a ruler of the synagogue	*Alex Thurley-Ratcliff*
Philip of Bethsaida	*Ralph Jessop*	**Talitha** daughter of Jairus	*Mary Barlow*
Nathanael Bartholomew	*Michael Beurlen*	**Priest**	*Adrian Jones*
Thomas Didymus	*Jonathan Mutton*	**Pharisee Elder**	*Malcolm Bruce*
Matthew Levi a tax collector	*Nigel Close*	**Sadducee**	*David Hook*
Simon the Zealot	*Peter Whitmarsh*	**Temple Guard Leader**	*Tim Robbins*
Jude (Judas son of James)	*Rob James*	**Temple Guards**	*John Launder*
James the Younger	*Tim Jordan*		*Stephen Jarvis*
Judas Iscariot	*Stephen Gleed*		*Martin Healey*
Pontius Pilate Roman Imperial Governor of Judea	*Mike Carson*	**Crowd leaders**	*Lou Lewis,* *Gloria Lewis*
Claudia Procula his wife	*Christine Philpin*	**Rita**	*Lynda Muncaster*
Pilate's Aide	*Richard Roope*	**Rachel**	*Anne Bennett*
Pilate's Attendant	*Sue Spurling*	**Simon of Cyrene**	*Neil Maddock*
Commander	*Paul Haycock*	**Rufus & Alex** his sons	*Harry Anderson*
Sergeant Major	*Rupert Cazalet*		*Alex Pellatt*
Corporal	*Babs Anjorin*	**Hermas** a friend	*Chris Gleed*
Soldiers	*Mark Williams*	**Yeshua Barabbas** a freedom-fighter	*Marcus Chapman*
	Nick Greene	**Dymas** a freedom-fighter	*Alistair McNaught*
	Robert Mundy	**Gestas** a freedom-fighter	*Michael Lewis*
	John Arthur	**Barabbas followers**	*Phil Clee*
	Bryan Boult		*Martyn Rollins*
	James Kirkwood	**Mary of Magdala**	*Polly Perry*
	David Thompson	**Mary** Mother of Jesus	*Angie Maundrell*
	Geoff Meads	**Mary** Mother of James	*Sue Higgins*
	Simon Irwin	**Martha**	*Theresa Smith*
		Joanna	*Christine Holmes*
Herod Antipas Tetrarch and Prince of the Jews		**Veronica**	*Lynda Price*
Herodias his wife	*Clare Carson*	**Miriam Clopas**	*Wanda Nash*
Salome daughter of Herodias	*Amanda Barnes*	**Serving women**	*Bethany Campbell*
Herod's Attendant	*Frank Goodland*		*Sian Woodruff*
Herod's Courtiers	*Sheila Wonnacott*	**Lazarus**	*John Le Riche*
	Ann Lee	**Gabriel** an angel	*Matt Honey*
Herod's Dancers	*Kylie Appleby*	**Michael** an angel	*Tim Honey*
	Nicola Bobb	**The Stranger**	*Katy Watkins*
	Sarah Haddow	**Radio presenter**	*Tim Daykin*
	Emily Moore	**Newsreader**	*Aimi Moignard*
	Emily Nunn		

Pundit	*Mike Perry*
Master of Ceremonies	*Michael Orpen-Palmer*
Expert	*Michael Scott-Joynt*
'Good Shepherd'	*Tommy Jessop*
'Banner Dancer'	*Rebecca McGee*
Fanfare Trumpeters	*Andy Thompson and Ed Fry*

'Louisa' and 'Waggledance' (the donkeys) were kindly provided by Wendy and Ray Andrews

BBC Radio Solent's live coverage of the three-hour event won the Jerusalem Award 2008, sponsored by the Jerusalem Trust. Very special thanks to the BBC radio team which included . . .
Presenter: Tim Daykin; *Reporters*: Joanna Lipsey and Matt Treacy; *Studio Presenters*: Tristan Pascoe and Dave Adcock; *Studio Producer*: Neil Sackley; *Outside Broadcast Engineer*: Malcolm Baird; *Editor*: Lisa Hardisty; *Executive Editor*: Mia Costello

The Winchester Passion Site Managers: Eddie Grimble, Tony Hellard, John Piper, Frank Roberts, Peter Russell, Derek Rutherford

Oram's Arbour Festival Team: Jane Bates, Kathleen Cook, Fiona Davidson, Diane Kingston, Juli Wills and the eager programme sellers

Steward Team Leaders: Ray Cousins, Rod James, Peter Kent, Ben Levings, Alec Martin, Julian Pringle and the many smiling stewards who guided people with firmness and grace

Technical Managers: Ken Liddell, Ray Lovegrove, John Shulz, Vince Smith, Thomas Swindells

Publicity team included: Sam Barnes, Heather Evans, Caron Greene, Jude Holt, Janet Jones, Gina Irwin, Alistair McNaught

Thanks to all those who with nimble fingers created the costumes.

TECHNICAL CREW & STAGING TEAM INCLUDED:
John Axford, Martin Aylmer Hall, Gary Aitkenhead, Babs Anjorin, Revd Marcus Bagg, David Bailey, Sam Barnes, Douglas Bennett, Carlton Bath, Lorna Browne, Lerys Campbell, Paul Carter, Ben Chase, Ed Chase, Thomas Chase, Nigel Close, Mark Cocklin, Christine Cook, Neil Ellis, Mike Farrell, Bob Forrester, Gareth Fox-Williams, John Garret, Daren Gibb, Frank Goodland, David Gover, Harry Harris, Mark Harris, John Heath, Stephen Herbert, Paul Hornzee, Trevor Hornzee, John Hilbourne, Mike Holt, Steve Jarvis, John Knapman, Will Law, Robert McNeely, Neil McSparron. Rob Mullane, Tony May, Yoko Nakamura, Mike O'Connor, Tim Padley, Rupert Pitt, Mark S Pyke, Steve Ray, Giles Richardson, Richard Ritchie, Andy Robinson, Howard Rowe, Tim Slatcher, Quentin Smith, Dan Sullivan, Nick Sullivan, Adam Swayne, Simon Swindells, David Teale, Jonathan Watkins, Jon Westmacot, Mark Wheadon, David White, Paul White, Adrian Whyte

WINCHESTER COMMUNITY CHOIR INCLUDED:
Angela Mwandia, Catherine Hahn, Cherry Giles, Chris Moran, Christopher Napier, Clare Flynn, Claudine Jones, David White, Debbie Germain, Erica Buckmaster, Frances Harrington, Gerda Patrick-Smith, Gerry Bracey, Helen White, Iris Gould, Jan Gapper, Janet Henry, Janice Openshaw, Jean Forster, Jeannette Archdeacon, Jonathan Cox, Kate Rolfe, Kay Borthwick, Meg Harrison, Mike Gray, Miranda Johnson, Paul Montgomery, Paul Northcott, Penny Ferguson, Robert Hutchison. Rosemary MacMullen, Sandra Roll, Sandra Thibault, Sheila Powell, Steve Cox, Terry Cooper, Wenda Moroney, Sarah Morgan

UNIVERSITY OF WINCHESTER GOSPEL CHOIR INCLUDED:
Minako Iwabuchi, Misa Suggi, Emma Hodge, Ai Hanagasaki, Helena Roberts, Elizabeth Taylor, Gina Marshall, Ali Frencer, Naomi Butchart, Charlotte Hamilton, Naomi Marsh, Nicola Rowles, Darren Alderton, Emma Shearmur, Jessica Brooks, Kester Lindley, Katy Gibson, Sam Cousins, Henry Watkinson, Matt Harder, Caine Morfett, Matt Gibbins, Jade Bascombe, Oriane Angelique, Hannah Williams

The world premiere performance of 'ADOREMUS: THE WINCHESTER PRAYER' by Sir John Tavener at the Winchester Passion 2008 featured members of the Waynflete Singers and Southern Voices.

WAYNFLETE SINGERS:
Soprano 1: Catherine Claasen, Beanie Devas, Eileen Dreyer, Christina Dumas, Clare Gardner, Alexa Heady, Sarah Jones, Jane Kennedy, Viv Lamplugh, Helen Longworth, Felicity McElderry, Lydia Parry, Christine Target, Sarah Walker

Soprano 2: Rosemary Brookes, Roslyn Clarke, Janet Evins, Stephanie Gretton, Liz Hake, Tamsin Hutchinson, Jan Meadows, Jane Moffett, Kate Poole, Sheila Redstone, Susan Rees, Veronica Shaw, Katy Violet, Anna Winter

Alto 1: Sophie Armstrong, Sue Armstrong, Heather Aspinall, Lynda Beckwith, Valerie Cork, Clare Criswell, Jenny Davidson, Susie Evershed, Ann Gildersleve, Gillian Jones, Sarah McWhirter, Susan Millin, Coralie Ovenden, Joanna Pankhurst, Rosemarie Roberts

Alto 2: Sue Sheridan, Brenda Sims, Rebekah Spanner, Kate Spencer, Liz Sweetnam, Anne Wiggle, , Funke Akiboya, Sue Batchelor, Kate Ball, Sandra Brown, Lara Buxton, Pamela Charlwood, Diane Dixon, Angela Garrett, Daphne Johnston, Jo Morris, Bridget Phelps, Lou Scott-Joynt, Clare Talks, Jessica Tringham, Rosie Whittock

Tenor 1: Piers Armstrong, Jeremy Bourne, Phil Ferris, Michael Payne

Tenor 2: Simon Acworth, Tony Gaster, Bob Howland, Martin Tomsett, Kevin Ward

Bass 1: David Billett, Richard Browne, Ian McAuslan, James Montgomery, Robert Normand, David Reece, Rod Stevens

Bass 2: Nick Caiger, Ray Carter, Arthur Davies, Duncan Eves, Edward Hepper, Allan Hill, Peter Meiklejohn, Chris Morris, John Sprott

SOUTHERN VOICES

Sopranos: Katie Alder, Claire Bentham, Olivia Brennan, Rebecca Brown, Rosie Collinson, Natalia Fetherston-Dilke, Francesca Harvey, Judy McKelvie, Debbie Mellors, Elizabeth Montgomery, Lizzie Nowosielska, Philippa Tucker, Sally Williams

Altos: Heather Corless, Julie Mutton, Beccy Read, Mandy Shaw

Tenors: Richard Anning, David Goodfellow, Sandy Lawrie, Phil Remington, Marcus Sangwine, Alan Turner

Basses: Ian Bentham, Steve Dean, Andrew James, John Lunt, Barry Marsh, Howard Nattrass, Alastair Nisbet, Richard Steedman, Pete Totterdel

CHRIST CHURCH WORSHIP GROUP included Nick Sims, Matt Howson, Steve Cutcliffe, Dave Payne

ST MARY'S CE JUNIOR SCHOOL performed songs by June Boyce-Tillman.

Staff: Marilyn Wright, Hannah Carter, Paula Osborne

Michael Ash, Jacob Bell, Luke Briggs, Matthew Briggs, Christopher Bryant, Oliver Clark, Harrison Crass, Charlotte Croft, Eleanor Davey, Charlie Davis, Rosie Duncanson, Harriet Fern,

Emma Filer, Emily Fitzgerald, Sydney Gayles, Lydia Grassi, Katie Guo, Callum Hawkins, Merryn Heels, Zara Hughes White, Daniel Hunter, Ryan Hunter, Georgia King, Rebecca Knight, Jordan Lewis, Eleanor McLean, Jamie McQuillin, Matthew Parry, Tash Porter, Daisy Potter, Owen Richardson, Molly Scargill, Alex Simons, Jorge Spicer Martinez, Jasmine Symonds, William Taylor, Tom Turner, Jordan Thorne, Amy Underdown, Holly Vary

MEMBERS OF 'THE PASSION CHORALE' INCLUDED:

Natasha Anderson, Caroline Andrews, Yazmin Barlow, Jenny Brown, Erica Buckmaster, Terry Cooper, Steve Cutcliffe, Victoria Devitt, Elizabeth Duff, Clare Flynn, Jean Forster, Debbie Germain, Cherry Giles, M Goodfellow, Lois Gravely, Michelle Harden, Paula Harris, Joy Hedges, Janet Henry, Alex Herbert, Allan Hill, Jude Holt, Naomi Honey, Robert Hutchison, Miranda Johnson, Lynne Jones, Pamela Jones, John Knapman, Moira Knapman, Hilda Lemon, Susan Lightfoot, Catherine MacManus, Rosie MacMullen, Peggy Mercer, Paul Montgomery, Christopher Napier, Shane Nickisson, Paul Northcott, Lois Price, Sandra Rall, Kate Role, Eileen Scoggins, Liz Slinn, Tim Stevens, Amelia Sweetland, S Thibault, Fiona Thornton, Brian Wakelin, Tricia Whitlock, Tony Wood, Lesley A Worrall

Every attempt has been made to include every person involved in the choirs, we apologise for any omissions or errors.

Ewen Huffman and Howard Mellor outside the Cathedral

The Winchester Passion

Written by Matthew, Mark, Luke, John, and Philip Glassborow
Script Editor: David Scott
Script consultants: Peter Russell & Paul McCusker

SOME NOTES ON THE SCRIPT

ROLES FOR WOMEN

One problem that concerned us greatly was the lack of female roles in the story. Jesus and his twelve disciples; Barabbas and his 'freedom fighters'; Caiaphas, Annas and all the priests, scribes and Pharisees; Pontius Pilate and his Roman officials and soldiers; Herod Antipas... so many of the leading characters are, by necessity, men.

We tried to compensate by inventing dialogue (where possible) for various female characters who are either mentioned or implied in the narrative.

Before Herod arrives to question the prisoner, his wife Herodias and step-daughter Salome step boldly into the chamber to see Jesus for themselves...

Pilate's wife arrives at the trial to warn her husband: 'Have nothing more to do with this good man...'

And Rita's Refreshment Van becomes the scene of a disciple's betrayal, providing roles for two tea-ladies who recognise Peter...

But perhaps our most radical invention was the character of The Stranger, a mysterious woman in red who mocks Jesus at the cross.

We also introduced some female roles which involved no dialogue, but which nevertheless carried great theatrical impact.

Lynda Price played Veronica, the woman who (by tradition) steps out from the crowd to wipe the blood and sweat from the face of her Lord...

Wanda Nash was able to fulfil her vision of portraying Miriam Clopas, a follower of Jesus who doesn't say anything but who loyally stays with him – and who leads the Daughters of Jerusalem in the video sequence...

Bethany Campbell was a graceful serving-woman who also played the flute during a scene-change...

And Rebecca McGee was our triumphant banner-dancer at the resurrection.

We were also able to set the tone of opulence and sensuality at Herod's court by seeing his dancing girls perform in front of sumptuous drapes hung in the Sculpture Garden. This gorgeous site-specific sequence was devised by choreographer Debbie Lee-Anthony of Winchester University with D@Win dancers Kylie Appleby, Nicola Bobb, Sarah Haddow, Emily Moore and Emily Nunn.

HERE IS THE NEWS

We used the device of a news broadcast at the beginning of the drama, to help set the scene. This enabled Tim Daykin – a BBC presenter in real life, playing a BBC presenter in our event! – to ask the 'reporters' on the ground, Aimi and Mike, about the political unrest in Jerusalem at Passover time.

Tim was also able to quiz an expert in religious affairs (none other than our very own Bishop of Winchester) about the background to the tension between Jesus and the Temple priests. Finally, he did a masterful job of ad-libbing as 'commentator' on various key points of the action.

WHO DO YOU SAY I AM?

In adapting the drama, I was struck yet again by the famous words of Jesus – 'But what about you? Who do you say I am?'

So in three key encounters with Jesus, I was able to find a place where he could ask precisely that question.

First, he asks two religious leaders – Joseph of Arimathea and Nicodemus – who are initially hostile to his teaching, but who eventually become secret followers.

Then he asks the High Priests Annas and Caiaphas, during his trial before the Sanhedrin. And finally he asks Pontius Pilate: 'Who do you say I am?'

(He doesn't ask Herod the question out loud, because Jesus declines to speak to him. But through his dignity and silence, he wordlessly invites the blustering prince to acknowledge his identity. And in that same scene, Herodias asks Salome: 'Who do you say he is?')

Jesus asks the question – even when he's on trial for his life – not for his own benefit, but for the good of the person he is addressing. It is purest grace, as he offers each person an opportunity to recognise who and what he is.

Shortly after writing this section of the script, I went to see The Oxford Passion, and was intrigued to find that its writer Lizzie Hopley had also picked up on this phrase. However, she dramatised it very differently. In her version, Jesus asked the question because he needed reassurance, affirmation. If people around him believed he was the son of God, that helped to build up his faith in himself.

Dramatically, that was a creative and interesting way to interpret the line. But for our Winchester Passion, it was another story. Our Jesus knew exactly who he was. He didn't ask the question to bolster his own faith, but to invite a response of faith from others: 'But what about you? Who do you say I am?'

BLANK VERSE

Readers will see on the page – although it was not noticeable in performance – that a few sections of dialogue are in 'blank verse'. The rhythmic pulse of Shakespeare and the Authorised Version, the cadence of iambic pentameter, seemed to work very well in certain scenes.

DIRECTORS AND CAST

Special thanks to the drama directors: Neil Simpson, Geoffrey Burnaby, David Simpkin and Dr Cecily O'Neill. They all made significant contributions in shaping the script during rehearsal,

trimming where necessary, and suggesting valuable additions. As indeed did several of our splendid cast, most notably Israel Oyelumade. Thanks to his inspiration, we added the two 'parable scenes' to help illustrate why the Pharisees and High Priests were so infuriated by some of Jesus' teachings.

Two brief sections of the script which were cut for time in performance are printed here in [[double square brackets]].

ACT ONE, SCENE ONE: Passover Preparations in Jerusalem

[For Jerusalem in Biblical times, read Winchester today. So for the arrival of Jesus – when he was acclaimed by the people calling out Hosanna – we needed a 'Winchester equivalent' of the festival atmosphere in the run-up to Passover.

We decided on a village fete at Oram's Arbour, with all the fun of the fair – yet overshadowed by the presence of the occupying Roman army. The Hamble Area Youth Band were playing; The Winchester Morris Men were dancing; The Passion Chorale were singing; children were performing a gymnastic display; clowns were clowning – yet all this happened under the watchful eye of the military, backed by a formidable array of weaponry, armoured vehicles and tanks.]

[AS PART OF THE FETE, THE PASSION CHORALE SINGS 'LET MY PEOPLE GO' (Words & Music: Traditional)]

SINGERS: GO DOWN, MOSES – WAY DOWN IN EGYPT LAND;
TELL OLD PHARAOH, LET MY PEOPLE GO!
WHEN ISRAEL WAS IN EGYPT'S LAND
(LET MY PEOPLE GO)
OPPRESSED SO HARD THEY COULD NOT STAND
(LET MY PEOPLE GO)
'THUS SPOKE THE LORD,' BOLD MOSES SAID;
(LET MY PEOPLE GO)
'IF NOT, I'LL SMITE YOUR FIRST-BORN DEAD
(LET MY PEOPLE GO!)
GO DOWN, MOSES – WAY DOWN IN EGYPT LAND;
TELL OLD PHARAOH, LET MY PEOPLE GO!

[THEN – at 6 o'clock – F/X: BBC RADIO SOLENT JINGLE]

TIM DAYKIN: Welcome to the six o'clock news with me, Tim Daykin. We're coming to you from Jerusalem, a city which is holy to the Jewish people, yet in a land – Judea – that's occupied by the Roman Empire. As you can see, we're in the build-up to a major Jewish religious festival, the Passover. Celebrations are going on all around – but nevertheless, there's a strong army presence in the city right now. What's the story here? Our reporter Aimi Moignard is on the spot. Aimi?

AMY: Thank you, Tim. Yes, preparations have begun for the Passover Festival, And for some background, I'm joined by our religious affairs correspondent, Mike Perry. Mike – can you tell us why there's so much tension in Jerusalem at this time?

MIKE: The Passover is a hugely significant festival. It's when the Jews celebrate being set free from slavery in Egypt – that's why they've been singing their old freedom song, 'Tell Old Pharaoh, Let My People Go'. However, today, many of the Jews are crying out once again to be released from oppression – this time, from the occupying force of the Roman army.

[[AMY: What do the Jewish people want? Do they expect the Romans to leave this country of Judea?

MIKE: It's a complex situation. The Jewish people are waiting for a king – or what they call their messiah, their deliverer. There are prophecies in their holy books. These writings foretell a king who will be sent from God to save them, like the famous warrior king David.

AMY: Is that the David who killed Goliath and defeated the Philistines?

MIKE: Yes, the shepherd boy who became king. The people believe that their new king or messiah will come in the name of David, and may even be a descendant of his.

AMY: So until this new king comes, how do they feel about the Roman occupation?

MIKE: Well, the religious authorities here – the high priests, the scribes and Pharisees – are willing to live under Roman rule, in order to keep the peace. But there are splinter groups among the Jews which refuse to accept military law. These groups are seen by some Jewish patriots as a resistance army, or as freedom fighters. But of course the Romans regard them as terrorists. So Jerusalem keeps erupting in violence, although as you can see, life somehow goes on as usual.

AMY: What kind of violence?

MIKE: Mostly guerrilla skirmishes against the Roman army, led by a famous freedom fighter, or terrorist, depending on your point of view, called Yeshua Bar Abbas. Everyone expects Bar Abbas to stage an attack at some point during the Passover celebrations.]]

MIKE: Ah, now this is very interesting. Look over by the city gates. Do you see the man on the donkey?

AMY: Yes – who is he?

MIKE: Quite a fascinating character. A local builder, a carpenter, called Yeshua bar Joseph.

AMY: Which means Jesus son of Joseph, is that correct?

MIKE: Indeed yes. The man appears to be completely self-taught, but he's gained quite a reputation among the villagers and country people as a teacher of the scriptures and a healer.

TIM: Amy – Mike – let me break in – we're going to get some pictures of this Jesus right now – let's go over to see what's happening. Cut to camera three, please.

[F/X: JINGLE INTO PALM SUNDAY HOSANNA SEQUENCE (Music by June Boyce-Tillman).]

[Jesus and disciples enter the city gates. Jesus is riding a donkey – children are singing – townspeople are shouting 'Hosanna, save us, halleluya to the son of David, blessings on the one who comes in the name of the Lord, hosanna in the highest. Praise God! He has sent us a redeemer! The king has come to us!' Crowd are throwing down their coats, branches, whatever before him. Pharisees yell out.]

NICODEMUS: Hey – you on the donkey – yes, you – tell your followers to shut up! These people are praising you as some kind of king! Calling out to you to save them!

JOSEPH OF ARIMETHEA: Tell them to be quiet! They're making an unholy row! Quick, man, shut them up!

JESUS: Don't you understand, you pharisees? If I told these good people to be quiet, then even the stones would cry out.

NICODEMUS: The little children are yelling, Halleluya to David's son! They're just children! They don't know what they're saying!

JESUS: Don't they? You teachers of the scriptures, haven't you read in the Psalms, 'Oh Lord our God, how excellent is your name – out of the mouths of babies and children, your Majesty is praised!'

JOSEPH OF ARIMETHEA: How dare you? How dare you speak to the religious authorities in this way? Who do you think you are?

JESUS: May I ask you something first? (DISMOUNTS FROM DONKEY) Who do you say I am?

JOSEPH OF ARIMETHEA: What? How should I know who you are?

JUDAS: Teacher, be careful how you speak to the Pharisees. They are powerful men.

JESUS: Judas, the time has come to speak plainly. How should you know who I am? Let me tell you. Because you have read in the prophet Isaiah, 'The Lord is coming to your rescue – and what will be the signs? The blind will see, the deaf will hear, the lame will leap and dance and those who cannot even speak will shout for joy.' Don't you see? These things are happening, before your very eyes. The dead are brought back to life and the good news is preached to the poor.

[JESUS WALKS AWAY IN CONVERSATION WITH NICODEMUS AND JOSEPH WHILE JUDAS AND OTHER DISCIPLES LEAD THE DONKEY OFF. WORSHIP GROUP SINGS '(PRAISE IS RISING) HOSANNA'.]

ACT ONE, SCENE TWO – FREEDOM FIGHTERS STRIKE BACK

[FX: JINGLE BACK INTO…]

TIM: This is Tim Daykin in the radio car – Amy – Mike – can you tell us what's going on here?

MIKE: It's fascinating, Tim. This man Jesus has entered the holy city on a donkey. By doing this, he is claiming to be some kind of king, or even the Messiah.

TIM: What – just because he's riding on a donkey?

MIKE: Yes, he'll be seen as fulfilling an ancient prophecy in the book of Zechariah. 'Shout aloud, oh daughters of Jerusalem. Your king comes to you, triumphant and victorious, but humble and riding on a donkey.'

AMY: But, Mike, why would a king ride into the city on a donkey?

MIKE: The donkey is a symbol of peace and humility. By riding a donkey, this man is saying that he comes in peace.

[F/X: JINGLE OUT]

PHARISEE ELDER: Move aside, there! Out of my way! Get these children out of it! Who's in charge here? Who was that man on the donkey? What's going on here?

JAIRUS: Why, don't you know him, Elder? That man is a prophet of God, Jesus from Nazareth in Galilee.

PHARISEE ELDER: Ah, it's you, Jairus. You say the man is a prophet? I've never heard of any prophet from Galilee.

JAIRUS: Sir, he has done many wonderful things. Healing the sick and making blind men see again, out in the country villages around here. You must have heard about him.

PHARISEE ELDER: What? You're the president of the synagogue,

JAIRUS, a man of position here – surely you don't believe such old wives' tales? Making blind men see?

JAIRUS: Sir, I have good reason to believe in this man Jesus. May I tell you this in confidence? My own beloved daughter, Tabitha, twelve years old – he went into the room where she lay dead. After a long illness. Dead. He took her little hand in his, and gently called her name, and she came back to life. It was a great miracle.

PHARISEE ELDER: A miracle? Then why were we not informed of this?

JAIRUS: He told us not to speak of it to anyone.

PHARISEE ELDER: Did he, indeed? You know that unless these things are reported to the religious authorities, and the evidence is examined by the chief priests, any alleged healing cannot be recognised as a miracle. It's not official until we say so.

JAIRUS: But, sir, official or not, I saw it happen with my own eyes. My own darling daughter. She was dead and now she lives! This Jesus must be a prophet, a man of God. Haven't you heard of him?

SECOND PHARISEE: Jesus of Nazareth? Oh, yes, we've heard of him – a builder, a common working man. A tradesman, a labourer with no schooling to speak of, a man who eats and drinks with prostitutes and outcasts, with corrupt tax collectors and with Gentiles – how could such a man be a prophet of the most high God?

[ARMY VEHICLES ARRIVE. CAPTAIN GETS OUT OF LAND-ROVER.]

CAPTAIN: What's going on here? Is this a protest against the rule of Tiberias Caesar? Or is it something to do with your Jewish festival? What is it, Pharisee – a religious ceremony of some kind? Or a political demonstration?

PHARISEE ELDER: Centurion, this is nothing to do with us. We are the authorised priests of the holy temple, and this man is nothing but a common builder from Galilee. A carpenter. His followers call him a Rabbi, a teacher, but he is not one of us.

SECOND PHARISEE: A Rabbi! More like a rabble-rouser if you ask me!

CAPTAIN: But your people were shouting out to him, saying 'Save us, hosanna!' What did they mean by that?

PHARISEE ELDER: Some people seem to think that he's a prophet, a holy man. These are simple people, and they may well be sincere, but they are surely deluded. There is always an upsurge of religious feeling at the time of the Passover Festival. It will all die down in due course. It was merely high spirits, nothing more.

SOLDIER: Captain! Centurions! Some unauthorised vehicles are approaching!

CAPTAIN: It may be Barabbas and his men! Look! Over by the city gate!

[A DISTANT EXPLOSION IS HEARD. DYMAS AND GESTAS RUN ON TO THE PERFORMANCE AREA]

GESTAS: People of the city! Now is the time to rise up against the Roman infidel!

DYMAS: Listen to the words of our heroic leader, Yeshua Bar Abbas!

[BARABBAS ENTERS]

BARABBAS: Hear what the Lord says in the Holy Book of Leviticus! I am the Lord your God… who brought you out of Egypt… to give you the land of Canaan and to be your God. People of Jerusalem! This holy city belongs to us! Kick out the pagan invaders, with their empty gods made of stone. The Lord our God is one God! And he gave this land to us, his chosen people.

[PURSUING JEEP HAS MEN SHOUTING THROUGH LOUDHAILER]

SOLDIER: Barabbas! Give yourself up! You are completely surrounded! Barabbas! Followers of Barabbas! Throw down your weapons! Surrender to the Roman soldiers!

BARABBAS: Never! I'll die before I surrender! I will be a holy martyr for God!

GESTAS: Death to the Romans! This land is our land! Leave us alone!

[FIGHT SEQUENCE. BARABBAS, GESTAS AND DYMAS ARE ARRESTED, RESTRAINED WITHIN OPEN 'PRISON CAGE'

ON TRAILER (LIKE CIRCUS CAGE TO CONTAIN A TIGER) IN CRUCIFIXION POSITION – WITH DYMAS AND GESTAS EITHER SIDE. TIM 'COMMENTATES' ON THE SCENE AS IT HAPPENS – THEN EXPLAINS THAT THE NEXT AREA OF ACTION WILL BE AT THE GREAT HALL. MUSIC PLAYED-IN ON CD – 'WAR OUT THERE' – AS STEWARDS LEAD THE AUDIENCE DOWN THE HILL TO THE GREAT HALL AREA.

PLAY-IN PRE-RECORDED VIDEO SEQUENCE TO COVER AUDIENCE MOVEMENT.]

TWO PARABLES

TIM: I'm here with religious expert, Michael Scott-Joynt. Can you give me some background, Michael, on why the Pharisees and Scribes are so angry with Jesus? What's going on here?

MICHAEL: He's got under their skin in a number of ways. He is reaching out to – and putting himself among – all kinds of people that they would see as ruled out of God's consideration. Prostitutes, outcasts, and what they would call 'people of the land' – common working folk, those who do the menial jobs, emptying the lavatories and suchlike. And of course, tax-gatherers – people who are doing the Roman's dirty work. Jesus is saying that God loves these people, too. And he goes out and spends time with them, sits down and has meals with them – which is not something the Pharisees would countenance with people they consider to be 'religiously unclean'. Yet this man has no formal qualifications – what gives him the authority for the things he says? He hasn't got the right letters after his name, as it were. What's more, Jesus tells a series of very demanding stories – we call them 'parables'...

TIM: Like the story of the Prodigal Son?

MICHAEL: Exactly. Some of these stories, these parables appear to be aimed at the religious leaders.

(CUT TO JESUS TELLING A PARABLE TO PEOPLE IN CAFE)

JESUS: Here's a question for you. Two men go up to the temple to pray. One is a Pharisee who strides in bold as brass. Very pleased with himself. The other is a shady businessman – a tax collector who's on the take. Who fiddles the books, and keeps a bit back for himself. He slinks in at the back and stays in the shadows.

Well, the Pharisee stands up at the front and he says, God, I thank you that I am a Pharisee. And furthermore, God, I thank you that I'm not like that crooked tax collector. As you know very well, God, I am a good man. If I say so myself, a very good man. I fast twice a week, and I give away precisely one-tenth of my money, as your holy law commands. Thank you, God, that I am not an extortioner or a crook like – well, like some people I could mention. Amen.

But the tax collector stands at the back, all alone. He doesn't even dare lift his eyes to heaven. He bows his head in the shadows and says, very softly, God, be merciful to me, a sinner.

Well, that's not much of a prayer, is it – with downcast eyes – God be merciful to me, a sinner. After that fine long speech from the Pharisee! But here's my question for you – which of these two prayers most gladdens the heart of the Lord? I tell you, this is the prayer he loves to hear: God be merciful to me, a sinner. One day, the self-righteous ones and the proud ones will find themselves brought down low. But those who are humble will be raised up.

(CUT BACK TO TIM AND MICHAEL)

TIM: One of the parables of Jesus. Surely this kind of story must be seen as explicitly critical of the Pharisees?

MICHAEL: It is certainly unsettling for them to be 'named and shamed' this way in public. Especially when they are in a crowd of people who are not like them. Among the common folk that Jesus would say they are excluding from the possibility of responding to the message of God's love.

TIM: So is Jesus a trouble-maker?

MICHAEL: The way he is living, and the things he is saying, are profoundly challenging to the status quo. But his parables have many different layers of meaning. Another story he tells is of a lost sheep and the other ninety-nine who are safe in the fold. This could be interpreted by the religious leaders as really quite reassuring – they would naturally see themselves as 'those who are righteous and have no need to repent'. But this parable also has a challenge – or an invitation – for any who see themselves as outcasts, as the sheep lost on the hillside. The shepherd is searching for them, God is looking for them and wants to bring them home...

(CUT TO JESUS TELLING ANOTHER PARABLE TO A SMALL CROWD)

JESUS: The religious leaders don't approve of me. Here's what they say – 'A man is known by the company he keeps. And look at this man – he talks with the common working people! And people of no reputation! And foreigners! He eats and drinks with sinners!'

Here's a story about a shepherd who has a hundred sheep. One hundred! That's a good size flock. But he's a good shepherd and he keeps a careful eye on them. Then one evening, he notices there's something wrong. One of his sheep is missing. Poor little thing must have wandered away somewhere and got lost. So what does the shepherd do? Does he stay in the nice warm barn with his ninety-nine sheep who are safe? No – he's a good shepherd, so he goes out into the wilderness to search for the little one that is lost. He hunts high and low and then – can you imagine his joy – he finds his missing sheep. He picks it up and carries it home on his shoulders. And he calls all his friends and neighbours together and says, 'Rejoice with me! I've found my little sheep that was lost!' Well, that's just the way it is in heaven, too! When one person who's wandered away is found again, there's a celebration you can't even imagine. Joy in heaven because one sinner has turned back home again, even more than for the ninety-nine who are righteous and have no need to repent.

I'm a shepherd, too. My sheep know my voice, when I'm calling them home. But some of my lambs are out in the wilderness. You wandered away from the meadowlands, just a little way at first, and then further and further. Now you're lost in the grey wilderness, going round and round in circles. You've forgotten all about your shepherd, who is calling for you, searching for you. But if you hear my voice, today, my little lost sheep – then come back to me – let me pick you up and carry you home on my shoulders.

ACT TWO, SCENE ONE – A PARTY FOR LAZARUS

[A TAVERN COURTYARD. A REMNANT OF THE WORSHIP SINGERS ARRIVES WITH THE DISCIPLES AND JESUS, STILL SINGING 'HOSANNA']

JUDE (ARRIVING): Lazarus, my friend. It was wonderful! They threw down their coats and shouted Hosanna to the King! The others are on their way...

LAZARUS: Sit down and have a drink with me, Jude.

JUDE: Thank you. Dear friend Lazarus! I raise my glass to you! Here's a health to Lazarus!

LAZARUS: Who could have dreamed that you'd be drinking to my health!

JUDE: To Lazarus, who has come back to us! Who has come back to life!

LAZARUS: Praise the Lord!

ALL: To Lazarus! Praise the Lord!

[MARY MOTHER OF JAMES, JOANNA AND MARY MAGDALENE LEAD JESUS TO A SEAT. MARY MAGDALENE CEREMONIALLY BREAKS OPEN THE JAR AND POURS THE PRECIOUS OIL OVER JESUS' FEET. JOHN, PETER AND JUDAS WITNESS THIS STRANGE SCENE.]

JOHN: Joanna – what's going on here?

PETER: Mary? What are you doing?

JUDAS: This is disgraceful! Such extravagance! Precious oil of spikenard! This must have cost someone a fortune.

MARY MAGDALENE: Yes, Judas. Indeed it did.

JUDAS: What a waste of money. And look at this alabaster jar, broken. We could have sold it and given the money to the poor.

JESUS: Judas, the poor are always with us, and there will always be ways we can help them. But I will not be here with you much longer. Mary?

MARY MAGDALENE: Yes, teacher?

JESUS: You have done well. You had saved up this treasure for a special occasion. And in your heart, you knew the time had come to use it. But do you understand what you have done today?

MARY: No, Teacher...

JESUS: You have anointed me, to prepare me for my burial.

MARY MAGDALENE: Your burial? Oh, teacher, no...

JESUS: And this love you have shown me will be remembered always. You have done something beautiful, Mary.

[JUDAS EXITS ANGRILY.]

JESUS: We must make ready for the passover. Martha – you've been working hard all day. Now, we are going to help you – yes, Peter and John, too – all of us together.

[THEY ALL LEAVE THE STAGE AND ENTER THE GREAT HALL DOORWAY]

ACT TWO, SCENE TWO – DECISION TIME FOR A DISCIPLE

[JUDAS WALKS UP THE TEMPLE STEPS WITH A BAG OF MONEY.]

GUARD: Greetings, friend. Is this a donation you bring to the priests?

JUDAS: This is an offering of one tenth of our money – it is our tithe to the temple. For the poor. (TO HIMSELF, BITTERLY)

Because the poor are always with us.

GUARD: (TAKING IT) Thank you. You're one of the followers of this bloke Jesus of Nazareth, aren't you?

JUDAS: What is it to you?

GUARD: You look after the money, do you? Well, Jesus wouldn't want you to give money to the temple, would he? He calls the priests all kinds of names – hypocrites, and bloodsuckers, and a brood of vipers!

JUDAS: He believes in the holy law of God.

GUARD: Does he now?

JUDAS: The law says we should give away one tenth of our money. So we do. Whatever Jesus may say about the Pharisees and Sadducees, he believes in the law.

GUARD: And what do you believe, my son? Do you go along with all his new ideas? Like, If someone hits you, don't hit back – turn the other cheek and let them hit you again? Or like, Love your enemy?

JUDAS: I must go.

GUARD: A word of warning, son. You're in danger. The priests don't want any more demonstrations about a Messiah, a King. They're afraid the Romans will come down heavy and close the temple. They're going to arrest you lot. Get you out of the way. Why don't you leave town while you can? Or better still, do yourself a favour.

JUDAS: What do you mean, a favour?

GUARD: Turn yourself in. Grass the others up. You'll get off scot-free if you do. You'll even get a reward.

JUDAS: A reward? What for?

GUARD: For doing your duty to the temple. Look, all we need is some information. They want to talk to your Jesus. Have a word with him. Make him see reason.

JUDAS: They can talk to him any time they want.

GUARD: Not at Festival time. Not in public. Everyone's going crazy for this Jesus bloke – son of David, save us, Messiah, halleluya. We'd never get near him. The crowd wouldn't let us. No, it's got to be after dark, privately, somewhere out of the way.

JUDAS: What do you want from me?

GUARD: You're one of his mates, aren't you? You must know somewhere quiet he likes to go? Somewhere secret?

JUDAS: What if I do?

GUARD: Take us there. That's all we ask. Then off you jolly

well go. A free man. Don't you see? It's the only way to save yourself! We'll make it worth your while. One-way ticket, wherever you want to go. Witness protection scheme, the lot.

JUDAS: What would happen to Jesus, if I do this?

GUARD: What's that to you, my son, as long as you're in the clear? Hopefully he'll listen to reason – stop stirring the people up. If not, he'll have to face a trial.

JUDAS: Trial? For what?

GUARD: For the things he says! He has been heard to say to someone, 'Your sins are forgiven.' But only God can forgive sins. So he's making himself equal with God. That's blasphemy. And you know the penalty for blasphemy. It's death.

JUDAS: Death...

GUARD: Of course, if he's innocent, they might let him go. Trouble is, you never know with trials. See, if he goes down, you all go down. Bang. All except you, if you co-operate with us. Anyway, think it over, why don't you? Come and see me later, and tell me what you've decided. Meanwhile, please – take this as a down-payment.

JUDAS: But this is our tithe-money, our donation to the temple.

GUARD: Well, it was, yes. But now, it's the temple's donation to you, personally. Take it as an act of good faith.

JUDAS: An act of faith?

GUARD: And be careful, my son! Remember, you are in mortal danger.

ACT TWO, SCENE THREE – A LESSON IN FOOT-WASHING

THE DISCIPLES ENTER IN HIGH SPIRITS – IT'S PASSOVER TIME!

JESUS: Now, Simon Peter – the next thing is – I need your feet.

PETER : Sorry, Lord?

JESUS: Peter the Rock – I need your feet.

PETER: (TRYING TO UNDERSTAND) Ah, yes – when you say, you need my feet, are you really saying, you want me to go somewhere for you?

JESUS: Peter, my friend – just give me your feet.

PETER: (GIVING UP GRACEFULLY) Sorry, Lord, I don't know what you're saying.

JESUS: (GENTLY) Perhaps my words are hard to follow sometimes. But this time, there is no mystery – I simply need your feet. (PUTTING A TOWEL ROUND HIS WAIST) Literally. Both feet. (PICKS UP BUCKET OF WATER) I'm going to wash them.

PETER: What? You, Lord? But that is the job of a servant. I can't allow you, my master, to wash my feet.

JESUS: My dear friend, unless I wash you, we are not in fellowship.

PETER: (IMPETUOUSLY READY TO STRIP OFF TOTALLY) Then, Lord, don't just wash my feet, but my hands and my head and everything.

JESUS: (GENTLY STOPPING HIM) Dear old Peter the Rock. You are already clean – mostly clean. So it's only your feet that need washing, and then you will be clean all over.

PETER: (SITTING) All right, then – wash them, Lord, if that is what you want.

JESUS: It is. (HE DOES) There. That wasn't so bad, now was it? Won't you let me dry them, too? Good.

PETER: Thank you. (RISING FROM THE 'FEET' SEAT)

JESUS: Good. Now, John, one of the boys of thunder. Oh, yes, I need your feet, too. You may not understand all these things now, but you will understand in the days to come.

JOHN: (SITTING) Will we?

JESUS: (WASHING HIM) I promise.

JOHN: I look forward to it.

PETER: John – over here – I'll dry your feet for you.

(JOHN RISES AND MOVES TO PETER)

JESUS: Yes, Peter. Good. You're catching on. Now – where is Judas Iscariot?

MATTHEW: I haven't seen him for a while. Anyone know where Judas is?

JUDAS: (ENTERING) I'm here, Matthew. Someone looking for me?

JESUS: Yes, Judas. I am. I'm going to wash your feet.

JUDAS: (GUILTILY) Me? But why my feet?

PETER: The Lord is washing everyone's feet. It's not just you, Judas.

JESUS: And soon you have a journey to go, my friend. So it's only right that I should wash you, too.

JUDAS: (SITTING) A journey? What are you saying, Teacher?

JESUS: (WASHING HIM) You must make up your own mind, Judas. You must make your choice. (JUDAS RISES, HESITATES AND THEN STAYS IN THE ROOM) All right, then – James, the other son of thunder – you're next. (JAMES SITS) Do you see what I'm doing here? It's really very simple. You call me your teacher and your Lord, and you say rightly, for so I am...

JAMES THE ELDER: (RISING) Thank you.

JESUS: Andrew, brother of Peter – your feet please. So, then, if I am your Lord, and I am washing your feet, then what should you do? Look – your brother's getting the idea.

ANDREW: Yes – about time he learnt to dry up! (LAUGHTER)

JESUS: Philip, feet please. All of you, my friends – always be ready to wash the feet of others. (PHILIP IS READY) Many of you will be leaders in the days to come.

PHILIP: Leaders?

JESUS: Yes, Philip. Now. Matthew Levi!

MATTHEW: Oh no, you don't want my feet...

JESUS: I certainly do. Hand them over. (LAUGHTER) Out in the world, the great leaders often lord it over their followers, and expect to be waited on hand and – feet! (MORE LAUGHTER) But that is not our way. Is it, Nathanael Batholomew? Yes, you next.

NATHANAEL: (SITTING) Um – what is our way, Lord?

JESUS: Our way is to lead people gently, by serving them. Don't you agree, James the Younger? Your turn...

JAMES YOUNGER: (WORKING IT OUT) To lead people by serving them? (SITTING) And serving people to show that we love them...

JESUS: Yes, James! Did you hear that, all of you? Serve each other, too. Look after each other. Love each other, as I have loved you. Who's next? Simon the Zealot.

SIMON THE ZEALOT: (SITTING) But Rabbi, why do you say, love each other, as you have loved us? As if it's in the past somehow? Won't you always love us?

JESUS: Of course I will, Simon. Always until the end of time. Isn't it love, when a man lays down his life for his friends? But I will not be here with you much longer. Not like this. Now. Where is Thomas? Ah, Thomas.

THOMAS: (SITTING) You won't be with us much longer? Where are you going?

JESUS: Where I am going, you cannot follow.

MATTHEW: What's all this?

THOMAS: Why can't we follow you?

JOHN: You're going somewhere?

JESUS: Yes, John. And now Jude, son of James – that's it – a dozen disciples and two dozen clean feet Ah, yes, all done.

JOHN: We will always follow you! Wherever you go.

JESUS: You may follow me again in the days to come, but you cannot follow where I am going now.

PETER: Lord, you know me – I would follow you anywhere – even to prison – even to death.

JESUS: Peter, my friend, let me tell you. Before tomorrow comes, before the dawn chorus of birdsong and the crow of the cockerel, you will all run away from me.

THOMAS: (LAUGHING) All of us? Run away from you? By tomorrow? I find that hard to believe!

JESUS: Do you, Thomas? I tell you, it's the gospel truth.

PETER: Lord, even if everyone else abandons you, I will never leave you.

JESUS: But you will, Simon Peter. What's more, you'll even deny that you know me.

PETER: No, Lord. No!

JESUS: Three times, my friend, before the cock crows. But I have prayed for you that your faith will not fail you. Come now, for I have been longing to celebrate the Passover with you. But we must hurry.

[SERVING GIRL INDICATES PASSAGE OF TIME BY PLAYING THE FLUTE, AS THEY TAKE THEIR PLACES AT THE PASSOVER TABLE]

JESUS: This will be our last supper together.

MATTHEW: What? Are you going away tonight?

JESUS: One of you will betray me and I'll be taken away. But the scripture must be fulfilled. I am warning you before it happens so you will understand.

SIMON THE ZEALOT: We would never betray you, Lord!

MATTHEW: Not one of us! Not one of the twelve!

JESUS: (CALMLY) The hand of my betrayer is with mine on the table, even now. (TAKING THE BREAD) Blessed art thou, O Lord our God, King of the universe, who bringeth forth bread from the earth...

[JUDAS LEAVES THE ROOM]

JESUS: (BREAKING THE BREAD) My friends, take this bread and eat it. (PASSING IT TO ONE SIDE) This is my body which is given for you.

PETER: Lord, I don't understand.

JESUS: (PASSING THE BREAD TO THE OTHER SIDE) This is my body which is broken for you. (NOW TAKING THE WINE) Blessed art thou, O Lord our God, King of the universe, who makest the fruit of the vine. Drink this, all of you. (POURING THE WINE – PASSING IT TO ONE SIDE) This is my blood which is shed for you. (NOW TO THE OTHER SIDE) This is my blood which is poured out for you.

MATTHEW: What are you saying, Teacher? How can this wine be your blood?

JESUS: You will understand in time. Don't be troubled. I'm going to the Father now, to make a place ready for you, and I'll come and meet you and take you there myself. So – now you know where I'm going, and you know the way.

THOMAS: But we don't know where you're going, so how can we know the way?

JESUS: Thomas, Thomas, don't you see? I am the way. You'll come to the Father through me, with me.

PHILIP: So then, Lord, are you saying that you'll take us to meet the Father?

JESUS: Philip, have I been with you all this time and yet you don't know me? If you have seen me, you have seen the Father. My Father and I are one. He is in me and I am in Him.

JOHN: You came from the Father, and now you go back to the Father. Your Father is God.

JESUS: Yes, John. And now the hour has come. Father, I pray for these friends that you gave me, that they will be one as we are one. And I pray not only for these, but for all who will believe in me through their witness. Amen. Now – we must go, my friends.

JAMES: But we haven't sung a psalm...

MATTHEW: We haven't finished Passover.

JESUS: Passover is finished. From now on, you will eat this bread and drink this cup in remembrance of me. It is time. Will you come with me – a little way at least?

THOMAS: Where are you going now?

JESUS: To the garden.

PETER: The garden?

JESUS: Come with me now to the garden.

[THEY ALL EXIT THE SCENE BY ENTERING THE GREAT HALL DOORWAY.]

ACT TWO, SCENE FOUR – GETHSEMANE BLUES

[ON THE BIG SCREEN OUTSIDE THE GREAT HALL, WE SEE THIS PRE-RECORDED SEQUENCE FEATURING 'THE PASSION KIDS'.]

Jesus went out in the garden to pray:
He said, Father, tell me father, does it have to be this way?
But his Father didn't answer. His Father didn't answer.

He prayed in the garden of Gethsemane,
Can't someone else do this – or does it have to be me?
But his Father didn't answer. His Father didn't answer.

Jesus dropped down to his knees and prayed,
He said Father, help me Father, cause I feel so afraid.
But his Father didn't answer. His Father didn't answer.

Jesus prayed so hard there was sweat on his head,
He said Father, please send somebody else instead…
But his Father didn't answer. His Father didn't answer.

Jesus lay down in the dirt on his face
And prayed, Some other time, Father, some other place?
But his Father didn't answer. His Father didn't answer.

Jesus said, Father, I can face the pain,
But what if I never see you again?
But his Father didn't answer. His Father didn't answer.

Why was there no answer? He already knew the answer.
No-one else could do it. Who else could go through it?
It had to be this way, and it had to be today.

So Jesus stood up in Gethsemane,
And said, All right Father, if it has to be me,
So be it. So be it.

And his Father answered – just one word.

The saddest 'Amen' you ever heard
Was the Father's answer.

[JESUS ENTERS ALONE AND STANDS IN A SHAFT OF LIGHT TO PREPARE HIMSELF FOR THE ORDEAL AHEAD. THEN PETER AND JOHN JOIN HIM IN A MOMENT OF STILLNESS BEFORE THE OTHER DISCIPLES ENTER AND THEY ALL WALK TOGETHER INTO THE CENTRE OF THE COURTYARD FOR THE BETRAYAL BY JUDAS.]

ACT TWO, SCENE FIVE – YOU HAVE THE RIGHT TO REMAIN SILENT

[JESUS AND THE DISCIPLES WALK INTO THE 'AMBUSH' – JUDAS EMERGES FROM SHADOWS WITH THE PRIESTS AND TEMPLE GUARD NEARBY.]

PETER: Judas! Where have you been?

JUDAS: Teacher!

MATTHEW: Judas? What's going on here?

JUDAS: Teacher!

JESUS: Friend – do what you are here to do.

JUDAS: (WALKS UP AND HUGS HIM) Teacher. I am afraid.

JESUS: Ah, Judas, is this how you try to save yourself? (TURNING FROM HIM) You priests and guards of the temple. Who are you looking for?

GUARD LEADER: The man called Jesus of Nazareth.

JESUS: (STEPPING FORWARD) Yes. I am Jesus.

GUARD LEADER: (FALLING BACK) What was that? Careful now, he may be dangerous.

JESUS: I said, I am Jesus. If you have come for me, then take me, but let these men go.

GUARD LEADER: Very well, then. (TO GUARD) If he gives himself up, they can go free.

PETER: No! You're not taking him! (GRABS SWORD FROM GUARD) Keep back! What is he to you? Keep away from the Lord! (SWINGS THE SWORD – INJURES GUARD, WHO YELLS OUT IN PAIN)

JESUS: No, Peter. That is not our way. (GOES TO THE INJURED GUARD) Let me help you. (TOUCHES GUARD'S EAR AND HEALS HIM. TO THE DISCIPLES) Remember, my friends, those who take up the sword will perish by the sword. Now go in peace, all of you. Go!

[DISCIPLES SCATTER]

JESUS (TO THE GUARDS) But why have you come armed with sticks to arrest me, as if I were a bandit? When I was with you day after day in the temple, why did you not challenge me then? But now is your time, the time of darkness.

GUARD LEADER: (CUFFING HIM) Jesus of Nazareth, you will accompany us to the house of the high priest. You have the right to remain silent, but anything you say may be taken down and used in evidence.

ACT TWO, SCENE SIX: CHALLENGE FOR A ROCKY DISCIPLE

[RITA'S REFRESHMENT VAN IS PARKED IN THE COURTYARD, SELLING HOT DRINKS. REGULAR CUSTOMERS STAND NEARBY, DRINKING TEA. RITA AND RACHEL CHAT WITH THEIR CUSTOMERS THROUGH THE WINDOW.]

RITA: So, they've arrested him, have they?

CORPORAL: Yeah – the temple guard picked him up. Turns out he was a fake all along. An impostor. A fraud.

RACHEL: Really? The man from Nazareth? The teacher, Jesus?

CORPORAL: Oh, yes, I heard it from one of the priests in the temple. He was claiming to be the Messiah and all sorts of nonsense! Leading the faithful astray.

RACHEL: Maybe he was getting more popular than the priests.

CORPORAL: No, straight up, he was a con artist, apparently. Working on the Sabbath, breaking the rules of the temple, mixing with the low-lifes, you name it.

RITA: What a shame. I've heard him talking. I thought he was lovely.

CORPORAL: That's the sad thing about it. He fooled a lot of people.

RACHEL: A con man, was he?

CORPORAL: (LEAVING) They always catch up with these blokes in the end.

RACHEL: Serves them right.

RITA: Still and all. He never did no harm, did he? Well, I thought he was lovely.

PETER: Tea, please.

RITA: Yes, love. Milk and sugar?

PETER: Please.

RITA: That'll be fifty pence. Oh – you're one of his lot, aren't you? What's he like? Is he really a con-man? Cause when I saw him talking, I thought he was lovely.

PETER: Sorry? What are you talking about?

RITA: Jesus. Who's been arrested. You're one of his disciples, aren't you?

PETER: Me? No.

RITA: But I've seen you with him in the market-place.

PETER: No, I tell you. I don't even know the man.

RACHEL: Come off it. You're one of his best friends – you're with him all the time – what's the point of denying it? And you're from Galilee, like most of his disciples.

PETER: (LEAVING) I swear to God, I don't know what you're talking about.

[F/X: COCK CROWS, DAWN CHORUS OF BIRDS. PETER STOPS IN HIS TRACKS, SPILLS HIS TEA.]

RITA: Come on, then, Rachel. Did you hear the cock-crow? Time to shut up shop.

RACHEL: End of the night-shift. Halleluya. And another day dawns.

[THEY CLOSE UP THE VAN.]

CHILDREN'S CHOIR ON THE TEMPLE STEPS:
'WHEN YOU'RE FAR FROM HOME'
(Music and words by June Boyce-Tillman)
WHEN YOU'RE FAR FROM HOME AND YOUR HOPE IS GONE,
HOPE IS GONE, HOPE IS GONE,
MY STRENGTH WILL BE THERE, MY STRENGTH WILL BE THERE,
I WILL CARRY YOU IN THE FACE OF HATE
WHEN THE FISTS ARE CLENCHED, FISTS ARE CLENCHED,
MY LOVE WILL BE THERE, I WILL CARRY YOU.
IN YOUR GOING OUT AND YOUR COMING IN,
GOING OUT, COMING IN,
I'LL ALWAYS BE THERE, ALWAYS BE THERE,
I WILL CARRY YOU, I AM YOUR FRIEND.

ACT THREE, SCENE ONE – THE HIGH PRIESTS

[JESUS IS STANDING TRIAL BEFORE THE SANHEDRIN]

ANNAS: Tell me, now. What have you been saying to the people?

JESUS: Why do you ask me this? I have always spoken openly, out in the countryside or in the temple or the synagogue. If you have an accusation against me, why don't you call those who have heard me speaking to bear witness?

GUARD: How dare you answer the high priest like that? [GUARD HITS JESUS]

JOSEPH: But wait, Annas – he is right – it is not lawful to question an accused man in this way – if he stands accused of a crime, then you must call witnesses to give evidence. You must not ask him to condemn himself out of his own mouth.

ANNAS: Witnesses! Oh, we have witnesses a-plenty! High Priest Caiaphas! Call the witnesses.

CAIAPHAS: Members of Sanhedrin, the governing body of the Jewish people, I call upon you now to give your testimony against this man Jesus of Nazareth.

WITNESS ONE: He claims to forgive sins! He is a mere man and he is claiming to be equal with God! No man can forgive sins! Let him be stoned to death for blasphemy!

WITNESS TWO: He came into Jerusalem from the Mount of Olives, riding on a donkey. Clearly he was saying that he is Messiah. The people acclaimed him as the Messiah and shouted out Hosanna, and he did nothing to silence them. Blasphemy!

SADDUCEE: High priest Caiaphas, I heard the man say he would destroy the holy temple of God that was made by human hand and build it again in three days!

CAIAPHAS: Did you say that? Well, man? I demand an answer!

JESUS: Even if I answer your questions, will you believe what I tell you?

CAIAPHAS: You must answer us. You will answer us. Did you threaten to destroy the temple?

ANNAS: Do you claim to be the son of the most High? Who are you?

JESUS: Who do you say I am?

ANNAS: How dare you!

CAIAPHAS: Jesus of Nazareth, I call upon you now in the sacred name of the most high God to answer me. Are you the Messiah, the son of the Blessed?

JESUS: Yes. I am.

CAIAPHAS: Blasphemy! He utters the holiest name of God – 'I am'! Did you hear the blasphemy?

JESUS: And you will see the Son of Man sitting at the right hand of God.

CAIAPHAS: Silence! Blasphemy! (TEARS HIS ROBE) Sacrilege and blasphemy! Who needs any more witnesses! What do you say?

ANNAS: Blasphemy. The man is guilty and the man must die.

PRIESTS: The man is guilty and the man must die.

CAIAPHAS: Then take him to Pilate. Take him to Pontius Pilate.

ACT THREE, SCENE TWO – THE GOVERNOR'S DINNER PARTY

[PILATE IS INTERRUPTED AT A FORMAL MILITARY DINNER – EMERGES IN DRESS KIT WITH VARIOUS AIDES TO GREET THE PRIESTS]

PILATE: Representatives of Sanhedrin. What is the charge against your prisoner?

PRIEST: Procurator Pilate, there are many charges. In my own sight, this man has broken the Sabbath.

PILATE: Broken the Sabbath?

PRIEST: Governor, it is against our holy law to do any work on the Sabbath – Saturday is our sacred day of rest.

PILATE: I know that – but what work is he accused of doing?

PRIEST: This man deliberately, in full view of the synagogue, healed a sick person on the Sabbath.

PILATE: What? Then you should have been grateful to him for the healing, not angry about his breaking a petty rule. (TO AIDE) Is this man Jesus some kind of healer, a physician among the Jews?

AIDE: Not only among the Jews, Governor – one of our centurions went to ask for his help on behalf of a Roman slave who was dying, and the slave was completely healed.

PILATE: Ah, yes, I heard about it. So this is the healer. What does he use, herbs and medicines?

AIDE: No, Governor, he prays to a God – the God that he calls Father.

PILATE: He prays to a God? (TO PRIESTS) When you accused the prisoner of breaking your Sabbath… did he offer any defence?

PRIEST: It was outrageous, Governor. Blasphemous.

CAIAPHAS: He said to us, he dared to say to us, 'The Sabbath was made for man, not man for the Sabbath. The Sabbath was made to be a joy, not a burden – to bless man, not to break him.'

SADDUCEE: He claimed he would knock down our holy Temple! This man seeks to destroy our traditions, to destroy our cherished way of life.

PRIEST: This man eats and drinks with prostitutes and crooked tax collectors!

PHARISEE: He casts out demons – therefore he must be a demon himself! Or a sorcerer!

PILATE: Enough of this! Silence! What are the actual charges against this man?

CAIAPHAS: We have three, Governor. Our first is that this man has been perverting the nation.

PILATE: Item One, he is charged with perverting the nation. Charge is dismissed. Too vague and imprecise. Next?

CAIAPHAS: Secondly then, Governor, a specific charge. This man has been heard in public, forbidding the Jews to pay tribute to Caesar.

PILATE: Item Two, it is alleged that Jesus spoke out against the paying of tax to the Emperor. Certainly, this charge is very grave. It amounts to sedition against the state. Were you an eye-witness? Did you hear his actual words?

CAIAPHAS: No, Governor.

NICODEMUS: Excellency, I was there on the day in question. My name is Nicodemus.

PILATE: Let his name be noted.

JOSEPH: So was I, Governor. I am Joseph of Arimethea.

PILATE: Take down their names and these men's statements.

JOSEPH: Your Excellency, Jesus was debating in the temple with the priests, and they tried to catch him out with a question.

NICODEMUS: They said, 'Rabbi, we know that you always teach what is right, without fear or favour. Tell us,' they said, 'is it against our Jewish law to pay taxes to the Roman Emperor? Or not?'

PILATE: Well, how did the man respond?

JOSEPH: Jesus leaned towards them and said, 'Show me a silver coin.'

NICODEMUS: I was standing nearby, so I handed him a coin of mine – this very coin.

JOSEPH: He held it high and asked, 'Whose image do you see on this coin?'

NICODEMUS: 'The Emperor Caesar's,' they replied.

JOSEPH: 'Caesar's?' he said – 'Then give to Caesar what belongs to Caesar, and give to God what belongs to God.'

NICODEMUS: Then he gave it back to me. And here it is.

PILATE: So be it. Two witnesses agree that the charge is groundless. Do any other witnesses come forward? Very well, then, the second charge is also dismissed. The prisoner did not protest against paying tax to the Emperor. His reply was very diplomatic. Rather inspired, in fact. Next! Remember, now – this is your final charge.

CAIAPHAS: Thirdly, this man claims to be Messiah, a king – the king of the Jews.

PILATE: Item three, Jesus claims to be the king of the Jews.

CAIAPHAS: You will note, Procurator, that a claim of kingship has political implications. It has an impact upon Rome and upon the Emperor Caesar himself.

PILATE: Indeed, High Priest. I will consider this charge now. (TO AIDE) Bring the prisoner here so that I may question him. Now, then. You are the man Jesus?

JESUS: Yes, I am.

PILATE: And are you the king of the Jews?

JESUS: Is that your own question, or someone else's?

PILATE: What do you take me for, a Jew? Do you think I'm looking for a king? Who are you, man?

JESUS: Who do you say I am?

PILATEe: I'm asking the questions here. Your accusers say many things. One is that you claim to be a king.

JESUS: If I am a king, then my kingdom is not of this world.

PILATE: Not of this world?

JESUS: Or else my loyal subjects would be here, with an army, fighting on my behalf.

PILATE: (TAKING HIM ASIDE) So then you are a king – but of another kind?

JESUS: King is your word. My mission is to tell the truth about God. That is why I was born, why I am here. Those who are ready to hear the truth will listen to me.

PILATE: The truth! You must remember, I'm a politician. Tell me, will you, what is truth?

JESUS: I am.

PILATE: You are? What is your meaning? In other words, you speak the truth?

JESUS: I am the truth.

[[PILATE: You *are*? The truth... (STRUGGLING TO UNDERSTAND) Hmm. 'I am' is the name of your Hebrew God. So 'I am truth' means that God is truth. Is that what you're saying? Look, you're clearly an intelligent man. Co-operate with me. I'm the governor here, for Heaven's sake. I have the power of life and death over you! I have the authority to release you, or to have you beaten and flogged, or to kill you.

JESUS: Yes, you have authority, but only because it was given you from above.

PILATE: From Caesar, do you mean? Given from above? What

are you implying? Where does your authority come from? Don't you see I'm trying to help you? What are you, man?

JESUS: Who do you say I am?

PILATE: How am I supposed to know? My own judgment would be that you're no political threat to Rome. What harm have you done anyone? I can't for the life of me see why the priests are so angry with you.]]

PILATE: Hmm. (MOVING TOWARDS PRIESTS) Sanhedrin, I've examined the prisoner carefully, and I find no fault with him. He's a philosopher, a rabbi, a holy man, not a political prisoner.

CAIAPHAS: Governor, as High Priest, I demand that this criminal be punished. In our law, he is guilty and must die. But only you can authorize the death penalty. It is Passover and we must have this matter resolved before sunset. Make a judgment upon this Jesus of Nazareth.

PILATE: What's that? 'Jesus of Nazareth,' did you say? (TO AIDE) Surely Nazareth lies outside my jurisdiction.

AIDE: Indeed it does, Governor.

PILATE: So. Have them sound the fanfare, and take down this verdict. They want a judgment and they shall have one.

TRUMPETERS: FANFARE

PILATE: Hear the words of your Imperial Governor, Pontius Pilate, Procurator of Judea. The charge is that this man Jesus claims to be the King of the Jews. Therefore, it is a Jewish matter and does not directly concern Rome.

CAIAPHAS: Governor, I must protest!

PILATE: Your protest is noted, High Priest. Furthermore, you refer to this man as Jesus of Nazareth. Nazareth is in Galilee, which does not fall under my rule. So the prisoner is the responsibility of your Jewish prince, Herod, who rules Galilee by the grace of

the Emperor. Therefore, I will send the prisoner to Herod for judgment.

PRIESTS: No, Governor! Procurator, please, sentence the man to death, here and now.

PILATE: The Procurator has spoken. Prince Herod is here in Jerusalem for the Passover Festivities, and the accused will be conducted to him directly under Roman escort. Your Temple Guard will now transfer the prisoner into Roman custody. Very well. You are dismissed. (TO AIDE) Well, I'm glad to get that one off my hands. Let the Jewish prince sort it out – it's a Jewish problem, after all.

ACT THREE, SCENE THREE – THE THRONE ROOM OF A PRINCE

[MUSIC. SOME DANCING GIRLS ENTER TO SET THE SCENE OF HEROD'S COURT. AS THEY DANCE, HERODIAS AND SALOME ENTER CURIOUSLY TO SEE WHAT IS ABOUT TO HAPPEN, ATTENDED BY A RETINUE OF SERVANTS. THEN JESUS IS LED IN BY THE ROMAN SOLDIERS.]

HERODIAS: Look at him well, daughter. Is that the man?

SALOME: No, mother.

HERODIAS: But how can you be sure, Salome?

SALOME: I am sure. That is not John the Baptist, brought back to life. There is a certain likeness in the eyes, but no. (SCORNFULLY) You can tell your husband that he need not be afraid.

HERODIAS: My husband is the ruling Prince of Galilee. And your step-father. Show him some respect, Salome.

SALOME: Very well, then, dearest mother. Tell your husband his highness Prince Herod – this is not the Baptist, the prophet of God who was beheaded in our sight. You need not fear that he's come back to haunt you.

HERODIAS: Then who is this man?

SALOME: No-one can tell. Some say he is a prophet of the holy God, even greater than John the Baptist. Some say this is not a man at all, but a demon, because he can cast out evil spirits and work strange miracles. Others say that he is Messiah.

HERODIAS: But you, Salome? You have the gift of second sight. Who do you say that he is?

SALOME: He is a man, but more than a man. I can see no further than that. It hurts my eyes to look at him. Tell your husband what I said..

[HEROD ENTERS, CARRIED ON A LITTER, WITH TWO BODYGUARDS IN ATTENDANCE. HERODIAS CROSSES TO HIM AND SPEAKS WITH HIM PRIVATELY.]

HEROD: (DISMOUNTING) I see. Yes. Thank you, dear wife Herodias. Thank you, Salome.

(WALKING TOWARDS JESUS) So here is our guest! A prisoner

sent from His Excellency, the Procurator Pilate. The man of mystery we've heard so much about. The carpenter, the rabbi, the miracle-worker.

Oh, yes, we know all about your miracles. Water into wine! Quite impressive. My magicians don't know that one.

(TAKES UP A GREEN GLASS BOWL OF WATER FROM A PLINTH) Here is water – won't you do it for us now? Go on, prove you can do it. Change it into wine. (MOVING CLOSER TO JESUS) Say the magic words. What's the trick? How do you do it? Won't tell us? Nothing? (HEROD DROPS BOWL AND IT SHATTERS.) Fair enough. A good magician never gives away his secrets.

(CONFIDENTIALLY) They say that you can even raise people from the dead! Now that is quite a trick! Rather a dangerous trick, as a matter of fact. You must see it undermines our authority. I have the power to kill. 'Off with his head!' The ultimate sanction – the death penalty. Inconvenient people can be done away with. Problem solved. But what's the use of killing them off? If you're going to come along and bring them back to life?

Ah, but can you really do it? Really truly? Hmm?

This is a very one-sided conversation. Don't you agree?

No answer. Perhaps you don't like me very much. You called me an old fox once, didn't you? 'Herod, that old fox.' Yes, I was informed of it. It wasn't very polite of you. And yet you teach your followers to love their enemies. Don't you love me? Am I your enemy? Just because I killed the prophet John, the so-called baptiser? 'Off with his head!' Well, you didn't bring John back to life, did you?

Aha! A reaction! At last, I got a reaction.

Miracles are all very well. Prophecies are more dangerous. But now – now they are calling you a king. 'The King of the Jews.' How ironic. Because, of course, I am the king of the Jews – or the closest thing to a king we are allowed. (HUMBLY) But I am a

prince in the noble line of Herods. And I do have a throne. See? (SITTING IN IT) A royal throne. It suits me, don't you think?

However! If you are a king, then you should sit in the throne. (JUMPS UP AND OFFERS IT TO JESUS) Go on. Please. If you are my king, then take the throne.

Are you the king? Are you messiah? Reply to me, you – you Jesus. Show me some respect. Understand? I am Herod. I have the power to kill you. The power of life or death. 'Off with his ----!' I could order it, now. (CLAPS) Guards! For your silence, your insolence, I could kill you this moment!

(GUARDS COME FORWARD. HEROD GESTURES THEM TO STAY BACK)

What are you saying with all this silence? Am I not worthy of hearing your voice? But you are the famous preacher man, the mighty prophet. Have you no message, no prophecy for me?

So. You won't speak. Very well. Then do something! Are you a baptiser, too? Like your cousin John? (PICKS UP ANOTHER GLASS BOWL OF WATER) Here is water. Won't you baptise me? Take it, damn you! (DROPS BOWL AND IT SHATTERS)

My God. I've realised what it is. (MOVES CLOSE TO HIM, FACE TO FACE) You don't fear me. No, no – it's more than that. I've got it... You don't hate me. Hmmm? Why don't you hate me, preacher man? Is it possible you really believe all that nonsense about love? Is that it? (VERY CLOSE NOW) Do you love me, Jesus? (HE LOOKS IN JESUS'S EYES – AND THEN BACKS AWAY)

No! I forbid you to love me. I defy your love! (HEROD SLAPS JESUS ON THE FACE) Soldiers! Take this man. And...

And if he is a king, then we must dress him like a king! In purple. (HEROD DRESSES JESUS IN HIS OWN PURPLE ROBE) In purple robes befitting his majesty. And then, you'll take him back to Pilate. And Pilate can kill him. Or save him. What does it matter to me?

(TO THE SOLDIERS, BUSINESS-LIKE) Tell your Governor, this man is no Nazarene, no Galilean. Jesus was born in Bethlehem. So he comes under Pilate's jurisdiction.

(ANGRY NOW, AS HE LEAVES) Do you understand? This man is nothing to me. Take him away!

ACT THREE, SCENE FOUR – JESUS ON TRIAL

[JESUS IS LED BACK TO PILATE'S PRAETORIUM. PILATE ENTERS WITH THE CHIEF PRIEST AND SOME AIDES, FOLLOWED BY THE PRISONER STILL GUARDED BY ROMAN SOLDIERS.]

PILATE: My judgment is – the man is innocent.

CAIAPHAS: Would we have brought him here if he were innocent?

PILATE: Clearly your own prince Herod thinks so, too! He sent the prisoner back in a purple robe. Was that to mock his title, King of the Jews?

CAIAPHAS: We have a law, by which law he must die. He claims to be the son of the most High

PILATE (TO HIS AIDE, TAKING HIM ASIDE): What? The son of the most High? What do they mean by this?

AIDE: That Jesus is the son of God. Or claims to be.

PILATE: The son of a God? We have heard of such things among our Roman Gods. There are tales of the Gods having children with mortals. But can such things be true?

AIDE: Who can say?

[PROCULA ENTERS]

PROCULA: Guards, let me pass. Husband! Husband, I pray a word with you.

PILATE: Procula, wife. Of course. (WAVING ALL AWAY) Leave us a moment.

PROCULA: Have nothing more to do with this good man. Send him away, dear husband, send him home.

PILATE: I am the Governor here. My hands are tied. How can I say, I will not deal with him? I sent him to the Jewish prince for judgment – Herod returned him! I must give a verdict. Why do you plead for him – a Jewish prophet?

PROCULA: This man is something more. There's danger here Danger and power. All this was in my dream.

PILATE: I never knew you troubled by a dream…

PROCULA: It was an awful dream, a dream of blood. And water, crystal water changed to blood. This man was in my dream – it was his blood.

PILATE: They're crying for his blood. I'll have him flogged, Then I'll release him. They will have their blood And he will be set free. Now, go in peace.

PROCULA: (LEAVING) Have nothing more to do with this good man. Beware the water. husband, and the blood.

PILATE: Take the prisoner and have him flogged, then bring him back to me.

[SOLDIERS TAKE JESUS INTO PRAETORIUM. WE HEAR HIM BEING WHIPPED]

CAIAPHAS: No! Jesus must die! And if you spare his life, You are no friend to Caesar. He claims to be a king! And under Rome, we have no king but Caesar.

PILATE: If you're so anxious for this man to die, kill him yourselves.

CAIAPHAS: We don't have Rome's permission! The High Priest may not put a man to death. Only a Roman judge can execute.

PILATE: Silence for the verdict of the Governor! (TO AIDE) Have them sound the fanfare, and take down this judgment.

[TRUMPETERS: FANFARE]

PILATE: Hear the words of your Imperial Governor, Pontius Pilate, Procurator of Judea under Tiberias Caesar. I have examined the prisoner again and find no proof of any wrongdoing. Behold the man!

[JESUS IS BROUGHT FORWARD IN THE PURPLE ROBE AND CROWN OF BARBED WIRE]

PILATE: Here is the King of the Jews!

CAIAPHAS: You taunt us with this purple robe of state, this crown of thorns. We have no king but Caesar!

[PILATE TAKES THE ROBE OFF JESUS, SHOWING THE BLOOD AND WOUNDS]

PILATE: Prisoner has undergone a Roman flogging. Surely now you are satisfied? Centurions are thorough with their punishments. Now hear me, people of Jerusalem! Under the gracious rule of Rome, we not only permit you to celebrate your Passover Festival…

[RAGGED CHEER FOR THE PASSOVER]

PILATE: But furthermore, we grant a special dispensation in honour of your Passover lamb. Each year at this time, we release a prisoner to you. And so, I will set this Jesus free – as a symbol of the lamb. Behold your king!

[SOME CHEERS, SOME BOOS]

CROWD LEADER: Jesus is not our king! Flog him to death! We don't want this man – no, we want Barabbas! If you'll release a prisoner – then Barabbas!

PILATE: Barabbas is a terrorist, a murderer. This man's a healer, a philosopher. I find no fault in him. So I release him.

SUPPORTER: Yes! Let him go! The man is innocent!

CROWD LEADERS: No, we want Barabbas! Give us Barabbas!

PILATE: What shall I do, then, with your king Jesus?

CROWD LEADERS: We have no king but Caesar! He must die! He claims to be the son of the most High! Stone him to death! Kill the man! Crucify!

PILATE: My judgment is that he is innocent. But since you cry for blood, his blood's on your hands. Bring water in a bowl for all to see -

[ATTENDANT BRINGS BOWL OF WATER]

PILATE: Hear now the verdict of the Governor!

[TRUMPETERS: FANFARE]

PILATE: I wash my hands in public of this case.
So – ratify the sentence of the priests.
Release the murderer. Crucify the King.

[PROCULA SCREAMS AND POINTS. THE WATER IN THE BOWL HAS GONE BLOOD-RED. ATTENDANT DROPS BOWL, WHICH SHATTERS. BLOOD-RED WATER GUSHES FORTH.]

PROCULA: (RUNS TO PILATE) Beware the water, husband, and the blood.

CROWD LEADERS: Crucify the impostor – string him up –
Tear him to shreds and leave the corpse to rot!

PILATE: (WRITING) Wait! Here is the charge the prisoner must bear.

[PILATE HOLDS UP A SIGN, 'THE KING OF THE JEWS'.]

CAIAPHAS: Governor! Do not write, The King of the Jews.
But write, He claimed to be King of the Jews.

PILATE: (FIERCELY AS HE LEAVES) What I have written, I have written.

BARABBAS: (BEING RELEASED) No! Let me die the hero's death! Let me die a martyr!

CAIAPHAS: It is expedient that one man should die for the people.

BARABBAS: But they've got the wrong man! He's innocent! It should have been me!

ACT FOUR, SCENE ONE – THE VIA DOLOROSA

[OUTSIDE THE COURT, THE PRISONERS ARE MADE TO CARRY THEIR CROSSES ON THE LONG MARCH TO GOLGOTHA. THIS IS PERFORMED IN STRICT MILITARY STYLE, WITH A DRUM ACCOMPANIMENT.]

SERGEANT-MAJOR: Crucifixion detail! Prepare for the march to the place of execution. Prisoner Gestas, come forward to take up your cross.

GESTAS: What? I'm not carrying that. Why should I carry that? Get off me, you Roman scum.

[GESTAS IS MAN-HANDLED FORWARD AND FORCIBLY FITTED WITH A CROSS BEAM.]

CORPORAL: Shut up and carry it. Or you'll get yourself a flogging.

[GESTAS IS LED TO THE MIDDLE OF THE STREET BEHIND THE DRUMMER]

SERGEANT-MAJOR: Now. Prisoner Dymas, come forward to take up your cross.

[DYMAS IS PUSHED FORWARD AND IS FITTED WITH A CROSS BEAM. HE IS LED TO THE MIDDLE OF THE STREET BEHIND GESTAS]

DYMAS: Cor, this thing weighs a ton! Oy, mate – couldn't I have a lighter one?

CORPORAL: Don't worry. You'll manage it all right, with a little encouragement.

DYMAS: All right, no need to push, I get the idea.

SERGEANT-MAJOR: Finally. Prisoner Jesus, come forward to take up your cross.

[JESUS WALKS FORWARD OF HIS OWN VOLITION, AND IS FITTED WITH A CROSS BEAM. UNFORCED, IN SILENT DIGNITY, HE WALKS TO THE MIDDLE OF THE STREET, STAGGERS SLIGHTLY, THEN STANDS TALL]

SERGEANT-MAJOR: Now, prisoners all. Forward march.

[THE THREE PRISONERS BEGIN THE LONG AND ARDUOUS JOURNEY, ACCOMPANIED BY SOLDIERS AND A MILITARY DRUMMER. A MOTLEY CROWD ALSO PROCESS ALONG WITH THEM, SOME MOCKING, SOME SYMPATHETIC. AT A STRATEGIC PLACE ON THE HIGH STREET, THE SALVATION ARMY BAND JOINS THE PROCESSION, PLAYING 'JUST A CLOSER WALK WITH THEE'.]

ACT FOUR, SCENE TWO – HELPING HANDS

[AT THE BUTTERCROSS, THERE IS A RAISED SECTION OF STAGING WHERE THE PRISONERS ARE EXHIBITED TO THE CROWD.]

SERGEANT-MAJOR: (DISPLAYING THE PRISONERS) Here they are – Prisoner Dymas! Prisoner Gestas! Prisoner Jesus! Let this be an example to you all. (JESUS STUMBLES AND FALLS) Prisoner Jesus! (KICKING HIM) Get up, man. Get up! (LEANING DOWN TO CHECK HIM) Blimey, the man's hardly got a pulse. He's almost done for. Lost a lot of blood already.

CORPORAL: Well, we wouldn't have flogged him so hard, not if we'd known he was going to be crucified. It takes a lot out of you, carrying a cross.

[A WOMAN IN RED – THE STRANGER – STEPS TOWARDS JESUS]

THE STRANGER: So. You're not going to make it, are you? This mighty saviour? This king of the Jews? Ha! Look at him. He can't even carry his own cross.

SERGEANT-MAJOR: Someone'll have to help him – this is a dead weight.

SOLDIER: Well, don't look at me, sergeant – I'm keeping order.

SERGEANT-MAJOR: Then find someone!

SOLDIER: (TO CROWD) All right, then, any volunteers? Strong fellow prepared to help this prisoner carry his cross? Come on, come on, someone, anyone? Look sharp – we can't keep the gallows waiting.

[SOLDIER NOTICES SIMON AMONG THE CROWD ON THE BUTTERCROSS WITH HIS TWO CHILDREN]

SOLDIER: What about you? Yes, you, man!

SIMON: Me? No. I'm just visiting the city for the Festival. I don't live here.

SOLDIER: Oh, you're a tourist, are you? (IRONICALLY) Welcome to Jerusalem! What's your name?

SIMON: I'm Simon. I'm from Africa, from Cyrene, and these are my boys, Alex and Rufus.

SOLDIER: Right then, Simon of Cyrene. You. Give the prisoner a helping hand.

SIMON: But I'm looking after my boys.

SOLDIER: Yeah. Be a shame to leave them without a father, wouldn't it? So do as you're told and I'll spare your miserable life. Otherwise, you'll be carrying a cross of your own!

[VERONICA MOVES TOWARDS JESUS AND STANDS BEFORE HIM, TENDERLY WIPING THE BLOOD FROM HIS FACE. HE THANKS HER WITH HIS EYES.]

SOLDIER: Come on, come on, we've wasted enough time already. That's the ticket. Now. You help the prisoner to carry

the cross-beam, see? Yes – it's heavy, isn't it? All right, then, forward march!

[VERONICA TAKES CHARGE OF THE BOYS AS THEY ANXIOUSLY FOLLOW THEIR FATHER, SIMON OF CYRENE. THE PROCESSION MARCHES ON TOWARDS THE CATHEDRAL GROUNDS. THE GOSPEL CHOIR SINGS 'HE AIN'T HEAVY, HE'S MY BROTHER' AS THE AUDIENCE ARE LED DOWN THE HIGH STREET.]

ACT FOUR, SCENE THREE – THE DAUGHTERS OF JERUSALEM

[PRE-RECORDED SEQUENCE ON BIG SCREEN: WE SEE MIRIAM CLOPAS AND THE OTHER LOYAL QUIET FOLLOWERS FROM JESUS' POINT-OF-VIEW. AS HE TRUDGES PAST THEM WITH HIS CROSS, THEY LOOK AT HIM WITH SORROW]

THE VOICE OF THE DAUGHTERS OF JERUSALEM: He is going to his death, a good man, an innocent man. Yet he takes the time to talk with us, through his pain and his exhaustion. He turns to us with love in his eyes, those dear eyes that are streaked with blood and sweat. It is a great effort for him to speak, and yet he speaks to us, not about his own suffering but about ours. At such a time as this, he is concerned for us. His voice is very quiet, but we hear every word, those of us who follow him. We are the daughters of Jerusalem, the girls, the mothers, the old women, the voiceless ones. The women of the city who care for the babies and cook the meals and clean the houses and tend the sick and care for the dying. And what is he saying to us, the daughters of Jerusalem? Do not weep for me, he says – but let me weep for you and for your city.

ACT FIVE, SCENE ONE – THE EXECUTION DETAIL

[THE PROCESSION OF SOLDIERS WITH THE TWO THIEVES AND JESUS ARRIVES IN THE CATHEDRAL GROUNDS. THEN THEY ENTER THE CATHEDRAL AND MOVE UP, OUT OF SIGHT, TO THE BALCONY LEVEL FOR THE NEXT SCENE.]

MC: Take your places, now, please. The executions will begin shortly. Take your places, please, for the executions of the three

prisoners. The best view for the executions is directly facing the crosses. Come along, now, please. Roll up, roll up, for the entertainment! Yes, we've got three prisoners for you today – a terrorist, a thief, and a so-called Messiah! Hurry along now, please...

[FIRST SECTION OF THE WINCHESTER PRAYER SET BY TAVENER:

Lord Jesus Christ, I adore thee ascending the Cross;
I beseech thee that the Cross may free me from the thrusts of the devil.
Lord Jesus Christ, I adore thee wounded on the Cross;
I beseech thee that thy wounds may be unto the healing of my soul.]

[EXTERIOR – CATHEDRAL. THE BALCONY UNDER THE WEST WINDOW. TWO SOLDIERS ENTER TO PREPARE THE UPRIGHTS. THEN, ONE AT A TIME, THE PRISONERS ARE LED TO THE POSTS AND THEIR CROSS-BEAMS ARE AFFIXED TO THE UPRIGHTS.]

COMMANDER: Crucifixion detail! Bring up the prisoners now as I call them forward! Prisoner Gestas!

CORPORAL: Prisoner Gestas. Anything to say before sentence is carried out? Do you express remorse for your terrorist activities?

GESTAS: Never! Death to the Romans!

[AS THEY FIX HIS CROSSBEAM TO THE UPRIGHT, HE SCREAMS OUT IN PAIN]

CORPORAL: Shut up, will you? Or we'll make it even more uncomfortable for you. (FIXES THE ACCUSATION BOARD ABOVE HIS HEAD – 'TERRORIST') Right, then. Now, Prisoner Dymas. Are you going to give us any grief? Anything to say?

DYMAS: Since you ask. Any chance of a quick fag, before you string me up?

ACT FIVE, SCENE TWO – NOW THE GREEN BLADE RISETH

[TWO ANGELS STAND GUARD AT THE TOMB. THE THREE WOMEN ENTER.]

GABRIEL: Quem quaeritis in sepulchro, Christicolae?

MICHAEL: Who do you seek in the sepulchre, you followers of Jesus?

MARY MOTHER OF JAMES: Jesum Nazarenum crucifixium, o caelicolae.

MARY MAGDALENE: We seek Jesus of Nazareth who was crucified, you celestial angels.

GABRIEL: Non est hic, surrexit sicut praedixerat; ite, nuntiate quia surrexit de sepulchro.

MICHAEL: He is not here, he is risen as he foretold. Go and announce that he is risen from the tomb.

GABRIEL: Look! See? This is where you anointed his body for burial, where he lay dead in his graveclothes. But now, why do you seek the living among the dead? He is alive! He is alive!

MICHAEL: Remember how he told you, the Son of Man must be handed over and crucified, but on the third day he would rise again – he would come back to life. Go and tell the other followers! He is risen from the dead, just as he promised!

GABRIEL AND MICHAEL: He is alive! He is alive!

[MARY MOTHER OF JAMES AND JOANNA DEPART, BUT MARY MAGDALENE STAYS, DUMBFOUNDED AND WEEPING SOFTLY. JESUS ENTERS QUIETLY.]

JESUS: Woman, why are you crying?

MAGDALENE: They have taken away my Lord and I do not know where they have put him.

JESUS: Who are you looking for?

MARY MAGDALENE: Sir, where is Jesus, please will you tell me?

JESUS: Mary.

MARY MAGDALENE: Rabbi! Teacher! You are alive! How can this be?

JESUS: Mary, Mary, don't be afraid. I am going to my Father and your Father, to my God and your God. Go, tell the others I am risen from the dead!

MARY MAGDALENE: What if they don't believe me? I can hardly believe it myself, and here you are, before my very eyes!

JESUS: They will see me themselves, very soon. You can tell them, I will see you all in Galilee!

MARY MAGDALENE: In Galilee!

CHOIR ENTER SINGING 'KEEP YOU IN PEACE'

(Words & Music: Sarah Morgan)

SINGERS: WARM BE THE SUN THAT SHINES UPON YOU,
SOFT BE THE WINDS AS THEY BREATHE ON YOU.
SMOOTH BE THE ROADS THAT RISE BEFORE YOU.

KEEP YOU IN PEACE TILL WE MEET AGAIN.
MAY YOU HAVE SHELTER IN STORM TO HIDE YOU,
MAY YOU HAVE STARS IN THE NIGHT TO GUIDE YOU,
MAY YOU HAVE EVER A FRIEND BESIDE YOU,
KEEP YOU IN PEACE TILL WE MEET AGAIN.
DURING THIS, THE DISCIPLES AND FOLLOWERS ENTER ABOVE.
FINALLY JESUS STANDS AMONG THEM.

JESUS: Peace to you all. My peace I give you. And I will be with
you always, until the very end of time.

SINGERS: WARM BE THE SUN THAT SHINES UPON YOU,
SOFT BE THE WINDS AS THEY BREATHE ON YOU.

SMOOTH BE THE ROADS THAT RISE BEFORE YOU.
KEEP YOU IN PEACE TILL WE MEET AGAIN.
MAY YOU NOT LACK FOR GOOD BREAD TO FEED YOU,
MAY YOU NOT LACK FOR GOOD HOPE TO SPEED YOU,
AND FOR YOUR SINGING A HEART TO HEED YOU,
KEEP YOU IN PEACE TILL WE MEET AGAIN.

[BELOW, THE GREAT DOORS OF THE CATHEDRAL ARE FLUNG
OPEN AND JESUS WALKS OUT IN A BLAZE OF LIGHT, FOLLOWED
BY A TRIUMPHANT BANNER DANCER. AS HE STEPS FORTH,
MARY AND THE DISCIPLES GREET HIM JOYFULLY. THEY ALL
WALK TOGETHER OUT INTO THE WORLD AND INTO A NEW DAY.]

The Producers would like to thank all those who have supported the Winchester Passion financially and with gifts in kind, including equipment and manpower. The vast majority of the funding has come from local churches.

We would like to acknowledge the following major contributors:

Bible Society
British Army – 17 Port & Maritime Regiment
British Army Catering Corps
Bunty Newport Charitable Trust
Christ Church Winchester
City Electrical Factors, Winchester
ELAND Cables
Future Media, Christchurch
Immanuel Church
Jerusalem Trust
Leckford Estates (Waitrose)
Methodist Church Southampton District
Network Rail
Paul Lunn-Rockliffe Charitable Trust
Richard Steel & Partners
Royal Navy - HMS SULTAN

RLC (Royal Logistics Corps)
St Lawrence Church
St Peter's Catholic Church
Stagecoach
The Balfour Historic Museum Trust
The Barleycorn Trust
The Theodore Trust
The United Church
University of Winchester
Vineyard Winchester
Wessex Trust, United Reformed Church
Westminster Evangelism Trust
Winchester Baptist Church
Winchester Cathedral
Winchester Family Church

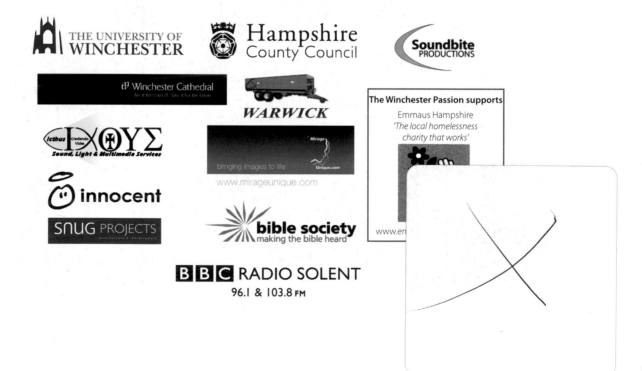